PRAISE FOR
# SACRED PSYCHIATRY

"*Sacred Psychiatry* is a breakthrough work of cosmic-sized genius. This book is an essential read for every person interested in including the realm of the cosmos into the dynamics of their health as well as the well-being of others. I love this book."

—**Caroline Myss,** author of *Anatomy of the Spirit* and *Sacred Contracts*

"*Sacred Psychiatry* is a unique and beautifully written book that is a bridge between many aspects of human illness and medical alternatives. Dr. Tsafrir has written a personal plea to the medical profession to open its heart and mind to new information and possibilities. The subjects covered in this book range from the author's specialty of psychiatry and mental health to the integration of that specialty with diet, nutrition, environmental exposures (including mold and EMFs), weaning from medications, mast cell activation, energy vampires, and a host of spiritual practices including astrology, the tarot, acupuncture, meditation, gemmotherapy, and limbic retraining. Dr. Tsafrir has done a masterful job of integrating these topics and making them completely relevant to those who are struggling to improve their health. This is a must-read for all of us."

—**Neil Nathan, MD,** author of *Toxic: Heal Your Body from Mold Toxicity, Lyme Disease, Multiple Chemical Sensitivities, and Chronic Environmental Illness* and *Healing is Possible: New Hope for Chronic Fatigue, Fibromyalgia, Persistent Pain, and Other Chronic Illnesses*

"Sane, balanced wisdom permeates every page of this brave book. Dr. Tsafrir takes you from your dinner plate to the stars while illuminating every link in the long chain that binds them together. In so doing, she shows us all a path to a better life. Even better, she knows that it's not the same path for everyone."

—**Steven Forrest,** author of *The Inner Sky, Yesterday's Sky,* and the Elements series: *The Book of Fire, The Book of Air, The Book of Water,* and *The Book of Earth*

"A truly inspirational book, a beautiful template for 'the medicine of the future.' Holistic and integrative in a profound sense with something for everyone, Dr. Judy Tsafrir's wisdom and deep experience shine through as she shares anecdotes from her own life and her work with patients. If you are on a journey of personal healing and/or spiritual awakening, this book is a gold mine of information. It clearly delineates the cosmic 'paradigm shift' and astrological patterns with which we are all currently engaging during these times of change and uncertainty which serve to reintroduce us to the sacred dimension of life."

—**Melanie Reinhart,** author of *Chiron and the Healing Journey; Saturn, Chiron, and the Centaurs*; and *Chiron, Pholus and Nessus*

"In *Sacred Psychiatry*, Dr. Judy Tsafrir offers cohesive models for healing in these times of unprecedented change. It is a wise, compassionate, and loving book that will benefit many for years to come."

—**Paul Selig,** author of *I Am the Word: A Guide to the Consciousness of Man's Self in a Transitioning Time*

"*Sacred Psychiatry* is a glorious book. What happens when a brilliant Harvard psychiatrist meets her inner wounded healer at 49 years old? She changes her life and embarks on a two-decade immersion into the holistic truth at the core of our being. In *Sacred Psychiatry*, Judy Tsafrir gives us her years of experience with a vast store of successful healing methods, both Eastern and Western. She reminds us that we all exist on several terrains, and that ailments which express themselves as psychiatric will always have multi-faceted causes. Her toolkit is vast, and every reader will come away with gifts and new understandings. She is not only a psychiatrist and MD, but also an experienced astrologer and shamanic healer who has integrated an understanding of the cosmos and deep nature into her tending of the body/mind/spirit. *Sacred Psychiatry* is for all of us as we confront our uncertain planetary future. It will be particularly enjoyed by psychiatrists and healers of all kinds. An inspiring, hopeful, and nourishing offering."

—**Carolyn Brigit Flynn,** author of *Communion* and
editor of *Sacred Stone, Sacred Water*

"*Sacred Psychiatry* marks the beginning of a new paradigm in the approach to mental health. Dr. Judy Tsafrir's courageous quest to understand human consciousness, to move beyond the prescription pad and couch, and to tenderly teach her patients the tools they need to reach inside themselves for deeper answers is profound. To be touched by the heavens as well as the earth, to call on our ancestors, and to listen to the drumbeat of our own human heart are just some of the ancient yet timeless processes offered within this brilliant and beautiful book. A generous work that will hopefully influence many fields for years to come."

—**Jamy Faust, MA and Peter Faust, MAc,**
constellation facilitators and authors of
*The Constellation Approach: Finding Peace
through Your Family Lineage*

"*Sacred Psychiatry* offers a visionary new approach to the healing of psycho-emotional illness. Inspired by Chiron, the wounded healer of ancient Greek mythology, Dr. Judy Tsafrir shares wisdom gleaned from her own personal healing journey as well as from her decades of experience as a clinician and teacher. Along with a wealth of ideas and that will open your mind and stories that will inspire your heart, the book is an invaluable guidebook of tools, practices, and readily available alternative medicines for body, mind, and spirit."

—**Lorie Eve Dechar,** author of *Five Spirits: Alchemical Acupuncture for Psychological and Spiritual Healing*, *Kigo: Exploring the Spiritual Essence of Acupuncture Points Through the Changing Seasons*, and *The Alchemy of Inner Work: A Guide for Turning Illness and Suffering Into True Health and Well-Being*

"Dr. Judy Tsafrir has written a book that lives up to its provocatively eye-catching title. *Sacred Psychiatry* is an exploration of the many ways in which psychiatry and American culture have gone astray by focusing solely on the material realm. She shows, in wondrous detail, how attention to the emotional, energetic, societal, and, most of all, spiritual dimension of life is the key to healing ourselves and our world. The reader can't help but resonate with her empathic case reports and self-disclosures and to learn from her vast range of knowledge and experience in an amazing variety of healing disciplines. A highly recommended paradigm buster!"

—**Eric Leskowitz, MD,** author of *The Joy of Sox: Weird Science and the Power of Intention* and *Sports, Energy, and Consciousness: Awakening Human Potential through Sport*

# AWARDS AND RECOGNITION

Nautilus Award, silver winner: health, healing, and wellness

National Indie Excellence Award, winner:
alternative health & psychology/psychiatry

San Francisco Book Festival, runner up: religious/spiritual

Eric Hoffer Award, honorable mention: spiritual

# SACRED PSYCHIATRY

Bridging the Personal and Transpersonal
to Transform Health and Consciousness

**JUDY SUZANNE REIS TSAFRIR, MD**

RIVER GROVE
BOOKS

This book is intended as a reference volume only, not as a medical manual. It is sold with the understanding that the publisher and author are not engaged in rendering any professional services. The information given here is designed to help you make informed decisions. It is not intended as a substitute for any treatment that may have been prescribed by your doctor. You should not begin a new health regimen without first consulting a medical professional. If you suspect that you have a problem that might require professional treatment or advice, you should seek competent help.

Published by River Grove Books
Austin, TX
www.rivergrovebooks.com

Copyright © 2024 Judy Suzanne Reis Tsafrir, MD

All rights reserved.

Thank you for purchasing an authorized edition of this book and for complying with copyright law. No part of this book may be reproduced, stored in a retrieval system, or transmitted by any means, electronic, mechanical, photocopying, recording, or otherwise, without written permission from the copyright holder.

Distributed by River Grove Books

Design and composition by Greenleaf Book Group and Sheila Parr
Cover design by Greenleaf Book Group and Sheila Parr
Cover images used under license from ©iStockphoto/Amiak and Allexxandar

Publisher's Cataloging-in-Publication data is available.

Paperback ISBN: 978-1-63299-920-7

Hardcover ISBN: 979-8-88645-114-6

eBook ISBN: 979-8-88645-115-3

First Edition

*To my mother and father and all my ancestors, and to my three children, Cam, Talia, and Yosef and all my descendants.*

The stars are like letters that inscribe themselves at every moment in the sky. Everything in the world is full of signs. All things depend on each other. Everything breathes together.

—PLOTINUS

I did then what I knew how to do.
Now that I know better, I do better.

—MAYA ANGELOU

# CONTENTS

**INTRODUCTION** . . . . . . . . . . . . . . . . . . . . . . 1

**CHAPTER ONE:** Reclaiming a Multidimensional Way of Being in the World . . . . . . . . . . . . . . . . . .19

**CHAPTER TWO:** The Current Astrological Weather . . . . .63

**CHAPTER THREE:** The Value of Astrology . . . . . . . . . .79

**CHAPTER FOUR:** Food Is Medicine . . . . . . . . . . . . 101

**CHAPTER FIVE:** Breaking Away from Energy Vampires . . 121

**CHAPTER SIX:** Weaning from Medications . . . . . . . . 141

**CHAPTER SEVEN:** Mast Cell Activation Syndrome, Mold Toxicity, and Ehlers–Danlos Syndromes . . . . . . . 157

**CHAPTER EIGHT:** Lions, Chiron, and Healing . . . . . . . 181

**ACKNOWLEDGMENTS** . . . . . . . . . . . . . . . . . . 189

**RESOURCES** . . . . . . . . . . . . . . . . . . . . . . . 191

**ABOUT THE AUTHOR** . . . . . . . . . . . . . . . . . . 195

# INTRODUCTION

*No matter who we are, no matter
in which part of the world we dwell, we are one.
We are one with each other. We are one with the Earth.
We are one with the moon, the sun, and the stars.*

—VUSAMAZULU CREDO MUTWA, ZULU LION SHAMAN

In 2013, a spell was cast on me when I encountered the white lions of Timbavati, in South Africa. I was there on a spiritual journey in support of conservation. While in Timbavati, we sought the lions out daily, both at dawn and dusk, and sat in the jeep for a long while and communed with them. I lost track of time in their presence. On one occasion, a male lion stood close to the jeep and roared and roared for an hour. I recall feeling mesmerized by his otherworldly presence and the primal sound of his roar. Over time, my feeling of connection with the lions has only strengthened. I evoke their guidance and protection regularly in my spiritual practice. The resonance that I feel with them is due to my recognition of the essential truth of the vital message that they bear in this epoch of increasing breakdown and collapse on the planet.

There were reports of sightings of white lions in the late 1930s, although their existence was not officially documented again until the mid-1970s. According to a legend of the Shangaan people of South Africa, the white lions are star beings, the most sacred animals on the African continent. In the ancient Shangaan language, *Tsimba-vaati* means "the place where star lions came down from the heavens." Timbavati, the region that shares this name, has been honored for centuries as a sacred protected area by African kings. It is located on the Nile meridian (31 degrees east), a ley line named Zep Tepi, and is believed to be the location where life first appeared on the Earth. Zep Tepi is exactly aligned with the location of the great Sphinx of ancient Egypt, the mythical creature with the head of a human and the body of a lion.

The Zulu legend recounts that the white lions originally appeared during the Ice Age in response to the people's desperate prayers and came to teach them how to survive, to hunt, and to keep warm in the extreme cold. After the danger had passed, they left but promised to return if humankind was ever in grave danger again. Now they have returned to Earth to deliver a message to humanity during these times of great crisis. Credo Mutwa, the late Zulu shaman, characterized this epoch on Earth as a time of both "catastrophes and real miracles." He viewed the reappearance of the white lions as a vitally significant fulfillment of the ancient prophesy and a harbinger of the time when humanity would either bow to the primacy of nature or go extinct. It is abundantly clear that this time is now. We are confronted daily with news of the evidence of the intensification of climate change around the globe. The destructive consequences of human activity resulting in the accelerated collapse of the planetary ecosystem are evident in the frequency, strength, and magnitude of storms, rising seas, flooding, heat waves, fires, droughts, and the loss of species, to name just a few of the devastating effects.

Linda Tucker, founder of the White Lion Global Conservation Trust, believes that the consciousness of the white lions is holding open a portal for humanity to connect more deeply with our divine nature. It does indeed seem like only through a radical shift in consciousness that acknowledges our kinship and interconnection with all that is will we be able to avert complete catastrophe.

## Destruction, despair, and doctors

We are living through a time of escalating structural global breakdown related to the fact that the current consciousness of our species is not one that honors, supports, and sustains life on the planet but rather is intent on destroying it. We have used our tremendous imagination and ingenuity to create weapons capable of annihilating all life on the planet while our air, water, and earth are being poisoned by corporations who pay off our politicians to support and protect their destructive practices. The economic inequality is staggering, with 47.8 percent of the global household wealth belonging to 1.2 percent of the world's population. The COVID-19 pandemic and its continuing consequences are also fueling a rupture with the world as we knew it. Those whose power is threatened are doubling down to enact laws to legitimize and fortify their rule and privilege, to sustain the existing patriarchal order that has brought us to this point of catastrophe and collapse.

In the face of the barrage of relentless frightening news, many people are suffering tremendous existential dread and hopelessness and are in desperate need of help. The available conventional psychiatric treatment approaches are frequently experienced by many patients as impersonal, inadequate, mechanistic, and even harmful. The standard of care employed by allopathic medicine and conventional psychiatry consists of making diagnoses via the identification of symptoms and diagnostic testing and then suppressing those symptoms with pharmaceuticals or procedures. The body is managed as though it were a machine devoid of consciousness, composed of different disconnected organ systems, to be treated by specialists trained to treat that specific part in isolation, to be tested, dosed with chemicals, or cut and irradiated. For any diagnosis, there is an algorithm that clinicians are obliged to follow or else risk disqualifying for reimbursement by the insurance companies. The pharmaceutical lobby determines much of the way medicine is practiced. At its core, our health care system is driven by a motive of profit, not public health.

Allopathic medicine takes pride in the standardization of care, and there is little tailoring of treatment to the individual. There is no appreciation of the innate intelligence and healing potential of the body, no emphasis on prevention or upon identifying treatable root causes of sickness, and certainly no place or acknowledgment of the power and reality of the central role of the sacred in healing. Western medicine has greatly reduced its capacity to heal by cutting itself off from this profound source of power and wisdom.

It's small wonder that many patients have very little trust in their doctors these days. They often do not feel known or cared for. The problem is a systemic one, and many doctors practicing conventionally are as unhappy as their patients. They are allotted insufficient time to spend with their patients and, during the appointments, interact primarily with the electronic medical record at the expense of establishing rapport. The system that determines the way conventional medical encounters are structured makes meaningful connection with patients, thoughtfulness, or creativity virtually impossible, as physicians are obliged to robotically follow treatment algorithms and are inundated with documentation requirements. It's unfortunately unsurprising that a 2020 study by the *Washington Post* reported that physicians die by suicide at twice the rate of the general population, given the fact that most went into medicine wishing to be healers but instead find themselves trapped in a soul-crushing predicament.[1]

## *The strengths and weaknesses of Western medicine*

The Western medical approach excels in the treatment of acute trauma, such as car accidents and gunshot wounds. It is also unparalleled for the treatment of conditions necessitating systemic stabilization in the context of an acute event, like sepsis, or conditions that require emergency surgical intervention, like appendicitis, bowel obstruction, or testicular torsion. It succeeds when it comes to elective surgeries to replace hip or knee joints or for surgical treatment of cataracts. Western medicine fails when it comes to the treatment of chronic conditions that are inflammatory in nature, such as cardiovascular disease, cancer, autoimmune conditions; or chronic mysterious illnesses like fibromyalgia, chronic fatigue, chronic Lyme disease; or illness caused by mycotoxins.

The crisis afflicting medicine and psychiatry is another expression of the much larger context of global breakdown, where the conventional approach to dealing with deeply rooted vast systemic problems is clearly not working. It's not an exaggeration to say that these are indeed extraordinary times, a threshold moment for humankind, where the world as we knew it no longer exists, but what is to come has not yet emerged and manifested in its new form. Technological developments have opened a Pandora's box of unanticipated implications. The splitting of the atom in 1932 and the subsequent development of nuclear weapons in 1945 created the possibility that, for the first time in history, humankind could annihilate itself. This is the most dramatic example

---

1 Marya J. Cohen, "Doctors Die by Suicide at Twice the Rate of Everyone Else. Here's What We Can Do." *Washington Post*, October 6, 2020, https://www.washingtonpost.com/lifestyle/2020/10/06/doctor-suicide-coronavirus-covid/.

of the devastating possibilities created by technological advances. But there are multiple other examples of the potential for destructive consequences related to artificial intelligence and the misuse of personal information, disinformation, health tracking, and genetic engineering to name just a few. These advances have created ethical questions that we do not have the wisdom to skillfully manage or answer.

## Separation

This is an in-between epoch of logarithmically accelerating change that is evoking tremendous uncertainty and fear. Some respond with denial, both of the magnitude of the losses already sustained and of the dangers we face as the biosphere is collapsing, millions of species are going extinct, and huge numbers of climate refugees are moving around the planet looking for both food and shelter. In the USA, vast numbers of people are addicted to drugs, more than half a million people are unhoused, there are ongoing attempts to subvert the electoral process and the rights of women, and regular grim occurrences of mass shootings, often of children in schools by other children, as well as racially motivated mass shootings in the streets, universities, houses of worship, night clubs, and stores. For many in the USA, there is an enormous and pervasive distrust of government, and no authority is considered legitimate. Rulings by the Supreme Court do not reflect the wishes of the majority of citizens. Fear and uncertainty translate into increasing polarization and susceptibility to belief in conspiracy theories. In the summer of 2022, I visited a flea market in Rogers, Ohio, and witnessed a large variety and quantity of paraphernalia related to anger at the government and threatening violence. There were bumper stickers, T-shirts, lapel pins, key chains, baseball caps, and signs to be displayed in front of the house, with variations on the message "We are angry, and we have guns."

It is a small wonder that people are depressed, anxious, and desperate for relief and reassurance. The anxiety and depression created by the national and global situation are driving people to seek help and, particularly, help that includes a spiritual component. Even when these external realities are not explicitly acknowledged, this is the desperate context in which the need for treatment is embedded.

Foundational to the loss of faith and disillusionment with allopathic medicine and conventional psychiatry is the prevailing scientific paradigm of seventeenth-century Newtonian physics and linear causality, of mechanistic cause and effect, and of separation in time and space. This model of separation pervades all aspects of modern Western society and culture and divides mind and body, spirit, and matter. It does not recognize what quantum physics has firmly established, that everything is interconnected and entangled. Space and time are categories of our perception, which can be effectively harnessed for feats of engineering and technological innovation, but they do not reflect the actual nature of the world as described by quantum physics, characterized by nonlocality and indeterminacy. Simply put, everything is connected, and everything impacts everything else. Furthermore, and most importantly in my mind, this model of separation creates a distinction between the divine and the mundane and does not recognize that the whole world is enchanted, alive, and filled with spirit.

The modern mindset has elevated and privileged the five senses and the rational mind to the exclusion of other capacities for knowing and understanding. It is utterly dismissive of a magical and symbolic approach to relating with the world. A mountain is a mineral-rich resource to be exploited for financial gain rather than revered as the abode of spirits, to whom you can express gratitude and also pray for guidance or assistance. An old-growth forest's value is measured as the quantity of timber it yields. Animals are treated as commodities rather than sentient beings we are in relationships with. It is this "rational" materialist mindset that regards the natural world as inanimate and separate from us that is at the heart of our extractive relationship and permits us to abuse and destroy the Earth as we do. This stands in contrast to an animistic worldview that sees the whole world as enchanted, all natural phenomena, including humans, animals, insects, plants, minerals, mountains, lakes, rivers, oceans, rain, snow, wind, all the elements—water, air, earth, and fire—as filled with soul and consciousness and therefore sacred. Animism also includes the belief that everything is interconnected. It is the spiritual foundation of the practices of indigenous cultures around the world.

## A holistic approach

Patients who come to see me are seeking healing that is holistic. They are extremely dissatisfied with psychiatry as it is conventionally practiced and are longing for a more natural and spiritual approach. They usually have seen several other practitioners before arriving at my office, often in a state of frustration and sometimes anger regarding their previous experiences with my colleagues. I am an adult and child psychiatrist and psychoanalyst, a shamanic practitioner, and an astrologer with a private practice in the Boston area. The patients who contact me are depressed or anxious, can't sleep or concentrate, but wish to avoid prescription medications. Some are currently taking psychiatric medications but would like to come off them, but their current psychiatrist is unwilling to help them to do this, or they were prescribed such a rapid schedule of tapering that it resulted in a severe withdrawal syndrome. Some have been exposed to toxic mold and wish to work with me because of my expertise in treating environmentally acquired illness. Some come to me because I am knowledgeable about the connection between autoimmune disease and psychiatric conditions and because of my familiarity with low-dose naltrexone, a medication that modulates the immune system but of which many conventional MDs are unaware. Some come because they are suffering from psychiatric symptoms related to long COVID for which prescription medications are not providing relief, and they seek alternative modalities. Some are drawn to me because they have had unusual spiritual experiences that they would be afraid to share with a conventional psychiatrist for fear of being considered crazy but have faith that I would not be so quick to jump to that conclusion. Some seek me out because of my training in astrology and the tarot and wish to incorporate those wisdom traditions into their healing journey or because of my training as an energy healer. Some simply wish to work with someone who has a more spiritual approach to healing.

Although most are longing for an alternative, holistic approach, they are reassured by the fact that I am conventionally trained and board certified in psychiatry. I am on the faculty of Harvard Medical School, which is where I did all my training in adult and child psychiatry at the Cambridge Hospital and where I continue to teach and supervise. My training in adult and child psychoanalysis has provided me with expertise as a therapist, so there is no need for them to seek out another practitioner for psychological work.

At the end of our first meeting, before my patient and I commit to working together, I make it explicit that our goal as I see it will not be a return to "normal." Normal is a state that is broken and responsible for creating the conditions that brought them to my office in the first place. Normal in 2023 in the USA is eating a diet of processed foods and regularly drinking alcohol; working long hours at a job that often does not feel like it feeds the soul and has little meaning or purpose; making minimal time for movement, fresh air, and sunlight; remaining indoors most of the time staring at screens; often living alone, having few or no close friends; having no sense of community or feeling of belonging; feeling out of touch with the natural world and the cycles of light and dark, as well as the night sky; and feeling totally disconnected from the ancestors and spiritual practice. This contemporary lifestyle is a powerful prescription for anxiety, loneliness, depression, and chronic illness.

## Our heavenly mandate

At this time of crisis and breakdown on the planet, the unique contribution that each of us was born to make is desperately needed. There is a Taoist belief that when the sperm and egg unite, a spark of starlight falls from the sky and illuminates the zygote. This heavenly spark contains the divine mandate for the individual, the entelechy, the vital guiding principle for this incarnation. My deepest wish is that the work that my patients and I do together will transform their lives and suffering and help them to embody their heavenly mandate. My patients and I work together to overcome the obstacles that are standing in the way of their realization of this goal. The work in my mind is not just about relief from feelings of anxiety or depression or returning to normal but also to get clear about why they are here, how they can contribute, and what are they meant to do with their lives.

Because I am not only a psychiatrist but also an astrologer and shamanic practitioner, those spiritual practices and mindset inform my work with patients. Astrology is a spiritual and holistic paradigm that uses archetypal language and posits that everything is connected and that events and experiences in our lives on Earth symbolically mirror the movements of the heavens, the cycles, and relative positions of celestial bodies. I have never heard a persuasive explanation of how astrology works, but my observation of the meaningful correlation between events in the heavens and life on Earth is repeatedly reinforced by my experience. There are many things in modern life that I depend upon and do not understand how they work, such as my car or the internet. Phenomena exist that are inexplicable now, but later, when scientific understanding has evolved, they will be explained. It would not surprise me if this will be the case with astrology as well.

C. G. Jung (1875–1961) was a Swiss psychoanalyst who coined the modern term *archetype*. The history of the idea of archetypes extends back to at least the ancient Greek philosophers with Plato's concept of eternal forms. Archetypes are primordial patterns or energetic templates that influence and even structure human psychology and behavior on many levels. Jung thought of them as universal primal energetic constituents of the psyche that are an expression of the collective unconscious. Archetypes are inborn categories of experience that have an essential, mythic, and spiritual quality that can be experienced both collectively and personally. Which planets will be particularly influential at a specific point in time is knowable, but the way an archetype will be expressed individually and collectively is not predictable. The same archetype can manifest in myriad different ways. For instance, an individual with the archetype of Pisces prominent in her chart could be someone who was motivated by spiritual seeking or could indicate someone with a vulnerability to addiction or possibly someone who had problems with addiction but who eventually healed through spiritual connection. Because the same archetype can be expressed in multiple different ways, it's not possible to predict what expression will manifest.

Shamanism is an ancient spiritual healing practice rooted in nature and is a way to connect with all of creation. It is based upon the assumption that there are helping spirits who are available to us to call upon for assistance in the healing work. My approach to my patients is not based solely upon my conscious rational mind and intention. Of course, I do run tests and make concrete recommendations based upon my training and fund of knowledge, but I simultaneously aspire to be a hollow bone, a conduit, and to allow the spirits to guide our work together. I always ask the spirits for assistance before I begin seeing patients for the day and give thanks after each session. I do not assume that the healing work is done by me, but rather, I am being guided and assisted as I try to help.

## Chironic psychiatry

I call this approach *Chironic psychiatry*. Chiron is an asteroid that was discovered in 1977. There is a correlation between the archetypal meaning of a newly discovered heavenly body with the zeitgeist of the time. In 1977, there was an upwelling of intense interest in holistic health, in Eastern medicine and the role of energetic and nonquantifiable factors in healing. The orbit of Chiron weaves between the planets Saturn and Uranus. Saturn is the most distant planet that was able to be seen by the ancients with the naked eye. Uranus is only visible with the aid of a telescope. Saturn signifies the cross of matter, embodied existence, bounded by space and time and knowable via our five senses, while Uranus represents transpersonal reality, only accessible through multidimensional ways of knowing. Chiron has been called the Rainbow Bridge, linking the personal with the transpersonal, matter with spirit, which is what I aspire to do in my work with my patients. Healing occurs when there is integration and balance of the body, mind, heart, and spirit with the Earth and the stars.

Chiron was a Greek mythological figure; there are numerous versions of his origin story. In one account, he was said to be the product of a rape. His mother, the beautiful nymph Philyra, changed herself into a mare to escape from the god Kronos, who lusted after her. When Kronos saw that Philyra had changed into a mare, he assumed the form of a stallion to impregnate her. When Chiron was born, Philyra was repulsed to discover that her baby was a centaur, with the body and legs of a horse and the torso and arms of a human. In her shame and disgust, she abandoned him. Thus, the circumstances of his origin and entry into the world involved tremendous trauma, both his conception by rape and, subsequently, the rejection by his mother.

The abandoned Chiron was found by a shepherd who brought the infant to Apollo, who adopted him and provided him with a broad education. He was taught medicine, astrology, divination, prophesy, poetry, and to play the lyre. Apollo's twin sister, Artemis, taught Chiron archery, hunting, and herbalism. Centaurs have a reputation as debauched, crude, and violent creatures. In contrast, Chiron was refined and highly educated and grew up to be a great healer and herbalist, a respected oracle and astrologer. Chiron symbolizes the reality that we have simultaneously an instinctual animal embodied nature represented by his horse body, and we are also divine beings who have huge imaginations, make art, and practice healing.

Chiron was revered as a mentor by many of the Greek heroes, and local kings would send their sons to be educated by him. In one version of the myth, his student Hercules accidentally pierced Chiron's thigh with an arrow dipped in the venomous blood of the Hydra, the nine-headed water serpent, which resulted in a wound that could not be healed and was the basis for Chiron's common moniker "the wounded healer."

The unhealable wound in his thigh caused Chiron unending misery, but as a demigod, he was immortal and could not be released from his torment by death. Despite all his expertise and knowledge of medicine, he could not heal his own wound. He was ultimately released from his agony by an act of sacrifice and service. He exchanged places with Prometheus, who, as a punishment for having given fire to humankind, had been chained to a rock, where an eagle came daily to peck out his liver, only to have it grow back again. The gods were so moved by Chiron's altruism that they freed him and placed him in the heavens as a constellation.

Like Chiron, we are all wounded. In this country, our wounds may be related to the vicissitudes of life in the family growing up, living in a capitalistic patriarchal culture with systemic inequality and racism, our religious upbringing, our experiences in school and the educational system, physical illness, loneliness, the lack of community and sense of belonging, and very importantly, our divorce from the natural world and a nourishing spiritual practice that connects us with the sacred dimension of life. All the wounds we received and our responses to them fuel our psychospiritual development and the potential for the realization of our heavenly mandate. I believe that it is my heavenly mandate to be a Chironic psychiatrist.

## My Chironic journey

I will tell you a bit about my origin story and healing journey. Like Chiron, I was rejected by my mother at birth. My father told me that, when my mother saw me, she declared that I was an ugly baby. She was very depressed during her pregnancy with me and, after I was born, went on to be psychiatrically hospitalized for a long time. Both my parents were German Jews, survivors of the Nazi Holocaust, and the shadow of that trauma was always present. My mother was the only surviving member of her family of origin and was never able to move beyond her grief and bitterness about the loss of her mother. She tried to end her own life many times. My father also lost multiple family members but not his parents. He responded to the terrible trauma by becoming very self-involved and grandiose. Trauma and heartbreak were very much a part of the everyday fabric of family life, so it was not surprising that my older brother chose a hearse for his first car and even purchased a second one! Consciously, this was not an explicit statement related to the family history, but to me, the determinants of this remarkable choice were unmistakable. The hearses were a concrete expression of the impact upon him of all the tragic losses my parents were endlessly grieving.

My father was a psychiatrist, a psychoanalyst, a professor of psychiatry, and a closet astrologer. He did not want anyone to know about his passion for astrology for fear of his reputation, but astrology was very important to him. He was a beloved mentor and had deep and intense relationships with many students. When he became older and required physical assistance, those who helped him with his personal care needs revered him. The public and private persona were very different. He was a difficult man to feel close to; he was authoritarian, competitive, and judgmental and was, at times, cruel, with little real empathy for his family. He had great difficulty seeing me or valuing me as a person, apart from my achievements. Since I could not be close to him, I became a version of him, at least professionally.

I married a man who shared many of the qualities of my father and had three beautiful children with him. The marriage was, however, unbearably oppressive, and in 2005, at the time of my Chiron return, when my children were still quite young, I separated from him, to protect both myself and them.

This concept of a planetary return is an essential one to understand, as it is very influential both personally and collectively. The duration of each planet's orbit around the Sun varies. It is common knowledge that the Moon travels around the Earth in 28 days, and the Earth travels around the Sun in 365 days. But all other planets also have orbits of varying lengths. For example, Jupiter takes 12 years to go around the Sun, Saturn 29, and Chiron 49. When an orbiting planet returns to the position it was in the sky at the moment of birth, the archetypal significance of that planet becomes magnified. It is not uncommon for patients to appear in my practice at the age of 49, at their Chiron return, as themes associated with their original essential wounding press upon the psyche for reconsideration and transformation.

Within three weeks of separating from my children's father, my own father died, followed by my mother three months later. This confluence of major losses prompted me to reach for the stars, and I consulted a professional astrologer, Nicoli Bailey, for the first time. It was such an extraordinarily affirming and remarkable experience—a stranger, through deciphering mysterious glyphs and symbols on a page, could see and understand me so profoundly—that I returned to see her every couple of months for the next several years to look at the birth charts of my children, as well as those of members of my family and friends. I finally resolved that I must learn to practice this art myself and undertook extensive courses of study with two well-known astrologers, Steven Forrest and Maurice Fernandez.

Up until this point, I had been practicing as a conventional psychiatrist and psychoanalyst for more than 20 years. After my Chiron return, I felt compelled to broaden my vision, to explore and incorporate a wide variety of holistic approaches to healing. It is not uncommon, at the time of the Chiron return, that a person experiences a desire to have spirituality play a more central role in their life. Over the next 15 years, I have explored many other healing modalities, practices, and wisdom traditions, including Buddhism, Kabbalah, shamanism, divination, plant medicine, herbalism, sacred activism, Reiki, Kundalini yoga, the Akashik records, nutrition, functional medicine, environmentally acquired illness, medical intuition, energy medicine, Ayurveda, and Chinese medicine.

I drew upon all these approaches as I metabolized and processed the considerable trauma and wounding that I experienced in my family of origin and that I went on to repeat in my marriage. After my Chiron return, I was drawn to explore therapeutic and spiritual modalities that also healed and transformed my own suffering. I have discovered that, like for Chiron, being of service to others has played a central alchemical role in my own healing. I have been blessed with the opportunity to offer to others the knowledge and wisdom accrued through my own experiences and heartbreak. The following chapters are a discussion of what I have learned and what I believe will support your healing process and resilience during these transformative times.

Meeting the white lions of Timbavati in 2013 was a part of that wide-ranging exploration. The encounter with the white lions touched me deeply—their beauty, majesty, and mystery, as well as what they represent mythologically. I heard the extraordinary extended roaring of the male white lion as a direct communication about the urgent need for us to shift our consciousness. He was commanding us to wake up and to listen, to shift our modern mindset of separation that denies interconnection and is reflected in our lack of love and respect for the natural world and our divorce from the sacred aspect of ourselves and nature. We must shift the paradigm from one of separation and scientific materialism to one that recognizes the sacredness and interconnectedness of everything so that we will be able to live in a way that supports the thriving of life on Earth now and for future generations. Only by doing this and by acting in accordance with this knowledge can we hope to bring about the changes that are so desperately needed.

## Playing your part

Writing a book about a holistic approach to healing poses the inherent conundrum of knowing where to begin. No one aspect of a holistic approach is more important than another. All the elements are necessary components to consider and are all vital constituents of the whole. Although the early chapters provide an overview of the astrological context in which we are all embedded at this point in history and a discussion of the value of an astrological understanding of people, this is not meant to signify that this is a book that is primarily about astrology. Similarly, any of the other crucial ingredients for healing from a holistic perspective, such as a daily spiritual practice, healthy nourishing relationships, diet, movement, and sleep, are not discussed in order of importance or priority. We are human beings with a mind, body, and spirit related to all other human beings, the natural world, and the cosmos, which lives within us, and we live within it. A deep awareness of this coexistence and interpenetration is essential to creating holistic health.

Fundamental to holistic healing is the fulfillment of your heavenly mandate. Pirkei Avot is an ancient collection of Jewish rabbinical teachings and maxims about living ethically. Rabbi Tarfon, one of the rabbis whose teachings are included in the Pirkei Avot said, "The day is short, and the work is plentiful; the laborers are lazy, and the reward is great, and the Master of the house is insistent. He used to say: It is not your duty to finish the work, but neither are you at liberty to neglect it" (Pirkei Avot 2:15–16). Although the current planetary situation can feel overwhelming, we are each called upon to play our small part, in whatever way is right for us, which will look very different for each person. Fame or prominence is not necessary. It can be of equal importance to be a good citizen, neighbor, parent, or friend. When we have done that, we may pass the baton to the next generation to continue the work. We need only do our part, there is no need to do it alone, and there is no need to finish the work. My hope and wish are that this book will provide courage, inspiration, and knowledge that will contribute to your holistic healing and that will empower you to do the part that is yours to do. As we are all one, our personal healing is inextricably linked with the healing of the planet.

*Chapter One*

# RECLAIMING A MULTIDIMENSIONAL WAY OF BEING IN THE WORLD

> One only sees what one looks for;
> one only looks for what one knows.
> —JOHANN WOLFGANG VON GOETHE

One of the foundational values put forth by the United States constitution is the separation of church and state, which was intended to guarantee religious freedom, allowing citizens to worship according to their own traditions and faith. Unfortunately, this mindset of separation has resulted in a mainstream culture that not only ignores and denies the presence and role of the sacred in our ordinary lives but also is, frankly, allergic to it, and the separation is at the heart of much of the suffering of my patients. Without a sense of themselves as spiritual beings, many feel alone, separate and finite, a body and a brain with a particular personal history that began at birth and will end when they die. They have no sense that they came here endowed with a heavenly mandate regarding their life purpose in this incarnation, that their consciousness will persist after the death of their physical body, and, equally important, that they are a part of and belong to the larger whole of the natural world and the cosmos.

This materialist secular modern worldview often results in experiences of existential dread, alienation, and hopelessness. Many do not have access to the sacred dimension of themselves or of the world around them and thus feel confined only to experiences of the world that can be apprehended with the five senses, rather than known through their intuition and heart. They have no practices, no familiarity with rituals or ceremonies that ground them and increase their sense of presence and attune them to a context larger than themselves, which provides a sense of magic, meaning, interconnectedness, and spaciousness. Without a sense of the sacred, they often feel depressed, anxious, and fearful as they slog through the dailiness of their lives, endure the inevitable changes, losses, and suffering associated with aging, sickness, and death.

This experience has been particularly heightened in the face of the massive planetary transformation that has been underway since 2008, when Pluto moved into Capricorn, and the collapse and transformation of long-standing hierarchical structures associated with the patriarchy began to accelerate.

The limiting mindset that is the prevailing paradigm of our culture is that if it cannot be scientifically proven, then it is not real. This mindset of separation is at the heart of the abuse, cruelty, and disrespect that we show each other and the natural world. There is a blindness to the reality that everything is connected and that, when we harm one another and behave in ways that are destructive to nature, we are simultaneously harming ourselves.

## Nurturing your spiritual life

A few years ago, in a talk at the 92nd Street Y in New York City, Rabbi Naomi Levy, author of a book entitled *Einstein and the Rabbi*, which is about reclaiming the soul, commented on the common practice of taking selfies in front of a gorgeous vista, where the self is featured large and the vista very much in the background. This focus upon the presentation and display of self is not a prescription for happiness. She recommended instead that we take a "soul-fie," which involves internally posing four questions daily:

- What has my soul been trying to say to me that I have been ignoring?
- What activities nourish my soul that I do not do enough of?
- What does my soul want to repair that my ego or vanity is too stubborn or fearful to repair?
- What does my soul want me to reach for?

These are profound questions that connect one to one's essence, the sacred aspect of the self. The rabbi commented that, when you listen to your soul, you are bold, and it does not matter whether others think that you are foolish or insane. You live in a way that feels true to your heart and that fosters a feeling of wholeness, alignment, and well-being.[2]

## "Normal" is a prescription for ill health and suffering

We think of the concept of "normal" as equivalent with healthy and natural, but so many of the conditions that we have become used to in

---

[2] Naomi Levy, "Learning to Take a 'Soul-fie' at Hanukah," *Hadassah Magazine* (November 2017), an essay adapted from her book *Einstein and the Rabbi: Searching for the Soul* (Flatiron Books, 2017).

modern society are normal in so far as they represent the average but are entirely divorced from the actual needs of human beings.

In our society, it is common to be lonely, and to have no sense of belonging or community. It is "normal" to feel chronically stressed and to work at a job that provides a paycheck but does not feel meaningful or fulfilling. It is "normal" to be obsessed with consumerism. It is "normal" to spend long hours staring at screens every day. It is "normal" to eat a diet that consists primarily of processed and packaged foods and to consume alcohol regularly. It is "normal" to have a sedentary lifestyle, to ignore circadian rhythms, and to not prioritize sleep. It is "normal" to take multiple prescription medications. It is "normal" to be totally divorced from the natural world and the night sky and to have no spiritual practice whatsoever. All these "normal" choices and practices are a prescription for chronic inflammation and ill health, alienation, and suffering.

It can be challenging and even scary to be different, to depart from "normal," to choose a lifestyle and values that are at odds with the dominant culture. The choice to be different than average can require courage but can contribute hugely to cultivating true health and resilience. Psychologist Abraham Maslow found that individuals who were healthier had a much more complex relationship with their less healthy culture and chose authenticity over fitting in.[3]

## Reinstating spiritual practice

When I meet a new patient, I always inquire about the spiritual dimension of their life. Very commonly, they grew up in families with no spiritual practice whatsoever, and they have absolutely no idea what it means to have a spiritually engaged life. Sometimes, they went to

---

3 Maslow, A. H., *Toward a Psychology of Being* (Princeton: D. Van Nostrand Company, 1962).

Catholic school and were obliged to attend Mass regularly, but it was a guilt-provoking, repressive experience, which they were only too glad to distance themselves from when they were free to do so. Their relationship to Catholicism only became more aversive and fraught as the revelations of widespread abuse of children by priests has become public and ubiquitous. Some patients were raised in homes that were culturally Jewish but had no connection with any sacred dimension of the tradition. Some were obliged to go to Hebrew school and to have a bar or bat mitzvah, but it felt empty and alienating and like they were going through the motions, rather than having an experience of a deeply meaningful developmental rite of passage in the context of the sacred community.

It is the rare patient in my practice who reports a rich spiritual experience in the family growing up, and many come to me with no personal practice as adults whatsoever. Some may meditate, but it's done with the goal of reaping the health benefits of relaxing the nervous system rather than as a practice that enhances consciousness, which can foster transcendence of the sense of the self as separate and enhance an awareness of the interconnectedness of all beings.

It can safely be assumed that the patients who I see are a self-selected group who are drawn to me because they are aware that cultivating the spiritual aspect of healing is central to my approach. When I ask a new patient whether they would be interested in having a more developed spiritual life, the answer is almost always yes. They have no idea about how to implement a spiritual practice but are very open and even hungry for guidance. In addition to ordering diagnostic tests and making recommendations for nutrition, sleep, movement, sunlight, and other lifestyle changes, my treatment plan always includes recommendations for ideas to create and cultivate a spiritual practice, if there is a desire for that. As our old world undergoes a rapid and thorough transformation, it becomes less and less possible to rely on external reality as a source of security. In order to remain resilient, it has become ever more essential to cultivate our inner psychospiritual resources.

## Spiritual tools

The following is an eclectic collection of specific spiritual practices that I have found particularly useful in my own life and that I recommend to my patients. All are easily accessible if you open your mind and heart and cultivate an attitude of curiosity, creativity, and playfulness. Some will increase your feelings of connection with yourself and others, peace, and openheartedness, and others will amplify your sense of enchantment and mystery of the world. All will support feelings of equanimity, spaciousness, and resiliency during these challenging times. Lengthy books have been devoted to most of these tools. I offer these short descriptions as a very brief introduction and suggest that you do more research into those that intrigue you. As it would be impossible to begin to do justice to the profound practices of yoga or qigong, I did not include them in this discussion, but recommend both regularly to my patients.

### *Altars*

I often talk with patients about setting up an altar in a corner of a room in their home to remind them of the soulful aspect of their being. Many like this idea. I suggest finding a beautiful cloth and assembling items that are meaningful to them. They may like to include objects that represent the four elements of Western astrology: earth, water, air, and fire. They could place a beautiful seashell to represent water that reminds them of a happy time at the seashore or a special rock or crystal to represent the earth element that has a metaphysical property that they would like to embody, a feather from a bird that has a meaning to them to represent the element of air, and a candle to represent fire. They could place a picture of a beloved person or pet on the altar, a vase with fresh flowers, a meaningful sculpture or figurine, or maybe a special beautiful bowl that they refill daily with water and ask for refreshment of their soul and healing of the waters of the earth. They could light the candle daily, reminding themselves that they are a spark of the divine, place their hands on their heart and feel the warmth, and spend just a few moments focusing awareness on their breath and affirming out loud, "I am embodied, and I am a multidimensional being." The altar is meant to uplift them, remind them of the spiritual aspect of their nature, and connect them with a feeling of spaciousness and to something larger than themselves. I encourage my patients to feel free to invent and to change their rituals as they learn different practices that speak to them.

Although it can feel like we are making it up as we go along, the more we allow ourselves to engage our organs of perception in this way, the more we come to feel that our making it up is divinely guided. *Making it up* implies that these practices are coming from us, through our own efforts and will, whereas *being guided* is allowing ourselves to be inspired by something beyond our own consciousness, allowing something to come through us. Given the rational, materialist conditioning that we have all grown up with in this culture, it is natural, when we engage in this unusual way, that it will feel like we are making it up. There is a need to consciously work with this conventional mindset, to liberate ourselves to be more available to experience intuition and inspiration and to trust our perceptions and impulses that are not based on the ordinary ways of knowing with the five senses. We undermine trust in our intuition when we denigrate this way of knowing and experiencing and characterize it as "making it up."

## Smudging

Smudging is a ritual practice that can be used for purification and for connecting with the spirits and guides. Fragrant plants, such as sage, palo santo, lavender, and sweetgrass, can be burned with the intention of connecting the earthly and heavenly realms via the ascending smoke. The burning plants can be passed over the body to cleanse the auric field. I like to spin clockwise with the smoking plant and affirm, "Old energy out" and then turn counterclockwise and affirm, "New energy in." This practice helps demarcate a new beginning and a fresh start. It can be useful to smudge before beginning to write or paint or engage in any creative task, asking for divine guidance and assistance as the smoke rises. If you cannot tolerate smoke or fragrances, smudging can also be done with sound, like with rattles, bells, or drums.

## Drumming

In some shamanic traditions, a drum is referred to as a spirit horse. Horses in many traditions are associated with power and are seen as messengers who travel to and from the spirit world. In many shamanic traditions, drums are used in ceremonies and rituals to alter consciousness, because they have the capacity to carry us to another dimension of experience. Brain waves entrain with the rhythmic sound of the drumbeat and can shift the consciousness from a state of everyday alertness to a more trancelike frame of mind.

A daily practice that I recommend to my patients is tuning into their spirit or praying while beating the drum. Many patients do not know how to do this. Annie Lamott, an author who writes about the writing process and spirituality, wrote a brilliant short guidebook to prayer called *Help, Thanks, Wow: The Three Essential Prayers*. Every prayer falls into one of those categories. I recommend drumming and asking out loud for help and guidance. You could ask for help and guidance with your health or the health of a loved one or with a project or challenging personal, professional, or financial situation. Ask for help regarding a social, political, or planetary matter. Drum and chant your thanks for all the many blessings in your life for which you are grateful. Drum and specifically express appreciation for the people in your life, for good things that have happened, for the ordinary magic of another day of life. Drum and acknowledge your awe and wonder at all the miracles and beauty that surround us. This practice helps you feel spiritually connected, and I do it every morning. I also like to drum before I meet my patients and to ask for guidance and help with our work together.

At the end of the day, before bed, drumming can be used to clear and cleanse the energetic field. The practice is as follows: Drum and ask that any energy that is in your field that does not belong to you be blessed and transformed and returned to whomever it belongs. Call back any energy of yours that has been left elsewhere and ask that it be blessed and transformed and returned to you. This use of the drum for resetting your energy can also be done after a disturbing or upsetting encounter or at any time when you feel in need of shifting your emotional state. Beautiful drums are readily available for purchase on Etsy, an online site where many craftspeople and artists sell their work. I have two drums that I use regularly. The smaller one is brown and speckled, with stars and painted with a white lion, and the other is large and a dark crimson color and has a very deep sound. It has designs in black of a snake and of the moon in all its phases printed on it. My drums are indispensable, beloved tools for me to connect with the spirits.

## *Offerings*

I talk with patients who are interested in developing the spiritual aspect of their lives about the practice of making offerings that I learned in my training with the Foundation for Shamanic Studies. We were taught that we are always surrounded by our ancestors and spiritual guides who want to be in relationship with us. Healthy relationships are not one-sided but, rather, are based upon reciprocity and mutuality. I learned that the spirits like to be asked for guidance and assistance—and preferably out loud. They do not interfere when they are not invited to help, and they like to be thanked as well.

One way to thank the spirits is to make offerings. An offering can be a handful of grain or lentils, herbs, or flowers. Really, anything will do. The intention is what matters. I often ask people if they have a special tree on their property or in a nearby park that they love. I have four trees in my garden, all of which have specific meanings to me, where I make offerings. In my backyard, there is a small purple parasol beech tree with coppery leaves that grows near the grave of my beloved dog Skugga. I often scatter my morning coffee grounds on the earth under this tree as I bless the garden and ask my dog for guidance. A sweetbay magnolia tree in the front yard blooms with fragrant, creamy white blossoms in June. I make offerings at this tree to the female ancestral line and to beloved women friends who have passed. A huge Leyland cypress tree is where I make offerings on behalf of the male ancestral line, and a rose of Sharon that is covered with pinkish-purple blossoms in the summer is where I make offerings in support of my creative self-expression.

I share my practices with you to inspire you to feel free to create your own rituals and ceremonies. I encourage my patients to invent rituals that feel soulful and nourishing and to improvise. I let them know that my own practice is endlessly morphing, but what is important is that it be done regularly. To strengthen the awareness of the sacred dimension of yourself and to cultivate a relationship with the spirits and guides, it is important to connect daily.

## Oracle cards

Oracle cards are wonderful divination tools that assist in the development of intuition and the capacity for self-analysis. They are different from tarot cards, which have a structure of 78 cards, four suits, court cards, and major and minor arcana. In contrast to the tarot, oracle decks are free-form and accessible to those who are naive to using cards for divination purposes, as they require no previous knowledge, memorization of meanings, or familiarity with the structure to use them effectively. There are literally thousands of varieties, with as many different themed cards with images, and they usually come with an interpretative guidebook. I have decks that are herb-, flower-, plant-, and tree-themed; animal decks; goddess-, shamanic-, and archetype-themed decks; and numerous other varieties.

The premise underlying the use of this oracular tool is that the cards that we select are not random but, rather, a way of accessing messages from the Universe that we are meant to hear. It is a sacred practice and should be done with consciousness that recognizes that this is a conversation with the divine. I usually light a candle and smudge, then shuffle the deck as I focus on the question "What does the Universe want me to know today?" I then pull cards from several different decks. I may just pull one card from each deck, or I may do a three-card reading, with the middle card representing where I am now, the card to the left representing what I need to let go of, and the card to the right being what I need to embrace. I look at the images, note what associations come to mind, read the interpretation, and then contemplate its message. Usually, the cards I pull from different decks will say the same thing in different ways, from slightly different angles, but there will often be a clear communication.

Sometimes, I pull a card that I do not understand. For example, yesterday, I was asking for guidance about a potentially challenging situation that I was anticipating, and I pulled a card that was called

Joy. Its placement was designated for the "what I need to let go of" position. I was puzzled. Why would I need to let go of joy? Joy seems like an emotion to embrace and invite into my life. In the context, however, of the other cards I pulled, I understood that the message was about letting go of the expectation of joy and not to be fearful that the challenging situation might bring suffering. If suffering occurred, it needed to be accepted. It reminded me that, sometimes, suffering cannot be avoided and that the art lies in meeting it skillfully.

I usually journal a bit about my insights from the cards and, in this way, tune into myself and spiritual guidance. Daily use of oracle cards and the remarkable synchronicities that occur regularly is one of my most cherished practices, providing both self-awareness and the awe and comfort of the repeated evidence that we are living in an enchanted Universe.

## *Crystals*

The use of crystals for healing is a tradition that has existed in cultures around the world since ancient times. Crystals are precious and semiprecious stones, each with unique physical characteristics that affect the human body's electrical charge and vibrational frequency, or *qi*. It is a form of vibrational medicine. Crystals also have associated metaphysical attributes and can be used in meditation and to support intentions. They can be worn on the body as jewelry or placed on an altar to symbolize the wished-for effect. Some examples are the use of rose quartz, a beautiful pink stone, to support the heart to open yourself to love. Clear calcite is used to empower intuition; labradorite, a dark blue-green-grey stone with iridescence is for protection, to amplify connection between the heavenly and earthly realms and to open yourself to magic and mystery. These are just a few examples. There are hundreds of different crystals, all with their own unique healing power and symbolism. Including beautiful crystals in spiritual practice can amplify a sense of connection with the divine. A wonderful resource for learning about crystals is *The Book of Stones* by Robert Simmons and Naisha Ahsian.[4]

## Holy basil

There are many powerful herbs from ancient traditions around the world that have venerable reputations for enhancing a sense of spiritual connection and expansion. I chose just one favorite to discuss here, but I encourage you to explore this rich and magical area. In the ancient medical tradition of Ayurveda, holy basil, also known as *tulsi* or *tulasi*, "the incomparable one," is considered the second most sacred plant after the lotus. It is an aromatic shrub in the basil family, belonging to the Lamiaceae or mint family.

This plant is worshipped as an embodiment of Lakshmi, the Hindu goddess of abundance and love, and is frequently planted around Hindu temples. A Hindu home is considered incomplete without a tulsi plant, where it serves both ceremonial and functional purposes. Its fragrant, volatile oils not only connect a person with the divine but also repel flies, mosquitos, and other harmful insects! It is thought both to protect the physical space where it grows and to promote prosperity.

Tulsi is classified as an *adaptogen*, an herb that helps a body adapt to stress and maintain balance or homeostasis. It is also one of the small number of herbs characterized as a *rasayana*, a renewing herb that supports the development of a state of perfect health, vitality, long life, and enlightenment. *Rasa* translates as "essence," and a *rasayana*, according to Ayurvedic practitioners David Frawley and Vasant Lad, "is

---

4 Robert Simmons and Naisha Ahsian, *The Book of Stones* (Heaven and Earth, 2005).

what penetrates and revitalizes the essence of our psychophysiological being."[5]

In Chinese medicine, tulsi is also revered as a Shen tonic, an herb that nourishes the spirit. It is a bioenergetic field harmonizer, which restores and balances our electromagnetic fields, balances the chakras, and helps clear out old, stuck emotions. There are different varieties of tulsi, but only three are medicinal: Krishna, Vana, and Rama. The Krishna variety has purplish-tinged leaves and is the most potent, Vana is found growing wild in India and Africa, and Rama is the most common cultivar in the USA. A calming, soothing, uplifting tea can be made from tulsi, by boiling two teaspoons of dried leaves in 16 ounces of water for five minutes. Fresh tulsi tea can be made by adding a quarter cup of leaves to one and a half cups of water and boiling for 10 minutes. It is mild-tasting and combines well with ginger, fennel, cardamon, lemon, and honey. Drink tulsi tea regularly to support both your immune and nervous systems and your spirit.

## Nature

Nature is a portal for connection with the sacred and has profound healing powers. There is abundant research demonstrating the beneficial physical effects of the natural world upon our organism, such as reducing stress and increasing the levels of serotonin and dopamine in our brains, both of which have a powerful antidepressant effect. The more time an individual spends in nature, the more they are likely to develop a sense of reciprocity and of belonging to a community of living beings, which is important medicine for the soul. It increases our consciousness of the need to protect the natural world, because there

---

[5] David Frawley and Vasant Lad, *An Ayurvedic Guide to Herbal Medicine* (Lotus Press, 2008).

is an organic recognition that the natural world is a part of us. Vitality is depleted by being indoors constantly, without breathing fresh air, feeling the wind and the warmth of the sun, and taking in the sights, sounds, and smells of the natural world.

Spending time outside at night is also tremendously healing. Light pollution in urban areas cuts us off from the majesty and mystery of the night sky. Many modern urban people rarely look up at the stars to experience their incomparable beauty. Our experience of ourselves is completely out of context and is another example of our divorce from nature and the cosmos, which has led to a distortion about who we are, our place in the Universe, and our responsibilities to each other and the planet. Astronomer Lucianne Walkowizc, in a TED talk titled, "Look Up for a Change," commented that we are so busy looking at our screens that we rarely look at each other, let alone the night sky. She described the night sky as a precious natural resource, like a park that we can visit, but if we do not protect it, it will slip away from us. If you care about protecting the night sky against light pollution, you could make a donation to The International Dark Sky Association, an organization that promotes this sacred mission.

## *Sunlight and animal messengers*

I talk with my patients about the importance of regularly spending an hour outside during the daylight hours. Morning sunlight activates the pineal gland, the producer of melatonin, which is particularly beneficial in regulating circadian rhythms and which improves alertness, metabolism, and sleep. It is preferable to walk in a place where it is possible to connect with the natural world, but if not, walking in an urban setting is better than staying indoors.

It is important to be present in the surroundings. Leave your headphones at home, and just notice the world around you and your thoughts. With so many interesting podcasts and YouTube videos, it is possible to endlessly listen to other people rather than to our own thoughts. Walking outside while being present promotes not only physical health but also our intuitive capacities.

Notice if you encounter any animals or insects on your walk. Each creature has associated archetypal symbolism. In a shamanic worldview, there is an underlying premise that the fact that this being crossed your path at this point in time is meaningful, and it carries a potential message to you from the Universe. There are a huge range of interpretations for each animal or insect, and I suggest first doing your own independent associative work before turning to a book or the internet. Examine your own thoughts and feelings and see what comes to mind. Once you are in the habit of doing this regularly, you may find that you develop your own unique language of interpretations that you associate with each creature.

When I do consult an outside source, I often turn to Ted Andrews's book *Animal Speak*. Here are some examples from his book. He associates turkeys with abundance and the blessings offered by the Earth. When I am walking and see a flock of wild turkey, I give thanks. Andrews associates squirrels with preparedness and activity. When a squirrel's presence is prominent in my field, I ponder what do I need to prepare or anticipate, or conversely, am I overpreparing, over-accumulating? Beetles are associated with transformation. If I notice a beetle, I think about what needs to change, what do I need to let go of, and what do I need to welcome into my life? These are just a few examples meant to stimulate your own process.

When we sleep, animal messengers can also visit us in our dreams and the same interpretive method applies. One night, I dreamt vividly of a creature that I could not identify. When I woke up, I instantly thought, "Could that have been a mongoose?" and googled "mongoose image." Sure enough, it definitely was! My only association to a mongoose was Kipling's "Rikki-Tikki-Tavi," which is a story about courage and fierceness. Embodying mongoose energy is about being a warrior, taking risks and following your vision undeterred by the opinions of others. The medicine of mongoose struck me as very timely and much needed as I anticipate the publication and promotion of this book that is self-revealing and so unconventional from a mainstream perspective.

I recommend cultivating a relationship with your waking life as though it were a dream so that you can appreciate that on a certain level, every encounter and experience is full of meaning that can be associated to and understood symbolically. My assumption is that the Universe is communicating with us constantly, and if we listen, there is a wealth of guidance and wisdom available. We just need to be open, to pay attention and foster this mindset.

## *Rituals to honor the new and full moon*

Awareness of the cycles of the moon is a way of attuning to and feeling connected to the rhythms of nature and to the cosmos. The new moon astronomically is when the Sun and Moon unite in the sky and is a time that is conducive to seed planting, both literally and metaphorically. Ceremony and rituals that include planting seeds and the setting of intentions is a way to honor and to harness the energy of this celestial event. Each new moon occurs in one of the zodiac signs and there is energetic support for intentions that align with the archetypal flavor of the sign of the new moon. For example, the sign of Aries is associated with boldness and pioneering. At the Aries new moon, intentions could be set to overcome fear and to dare to do something that you have longed to have the courage to do. Another example would be that the sign of Virgo is associated with holistic healing. A new moon in Virgo could be used to support the changing of health routines, an intention to upgrade the diet or initiate a new movement practice or improve sleep hygiene. You can look up the archetypal signification of the zodiac sign in which the new moon takes place in any basic astrology text or online and create an intention-setting ceremony that embodies its meaning. You may wish to create an altar for your ceremony on which you lay crystals, smudge using fragrant herbs, light a candle, drum and meditate in preparation for the ritual, drink a cup of tulsi tea to promote a feeling of spiritual expansion, and pull an oracle card for guidance.

The full moon occurs two weeks after the new moon, and astronomically is when the Moon and Sun are 180 degrees apart and opposite one another in the sky. The full moon is a time of maximum brightness and illumination, of full flowering of a situation, and that supports intentions of release and surrender. Ceremonies that embody the quality of letting go can be performed at this time. During a full moon ceremony an intention can be set to free oneself of limiting beliefs, to let go of destructive attachments in a relationship, and of anything that no longer serves and has run its course. There is energetic support to let go of anger at the self and others and to ask for forgiveness. What one wishes to release can be written down on a piece of paper and burned or cast symbolically into water or buried in the earth. Another possibility is to dedicate a journal to this purpose, and every month at the time of the new and full moon to record what you wish to manifest and what you wish to release. Practices that honor the new and full moons will help you to align with the cosmic energies and support you in your intentions and endeavors, as well as intimately connect you with yourself. Always remember to express gratitude at the end of a ceremony or ritual for the opportunity to connect with the cosmos in this sacred way. You may wish to make an offering.

## The Blessing Way

Angeles Arrien was a cultural anthropologist who studied comparative spiritual practices and shamanism. In 2014, a year before she died, she gave a wonderful TED Talk, entitled "Cornerstones of Wisdom: The Four-Fold Way." In it, she described a practice that she called *the Blessing Way*, which she derived from studying the spiritual practices of cultures from around the world and identifying the similarities between them.

Three practices were common to all of those that she studied. The first is prayer or setting a sacred intention. Some people are uncomfortable with the word or concept of prayer, but setting an intention feels less foreign and awkward. What is essential is to ask with heartfelt sincerity for assistance, guidance, or healing for yourself or another.

The second commonality is the expression of gratitude and appreciation for all the blessings in our lives. No matter how much we are suffering and how much we wish things were different, there is still always so much to be grateful for. There is a huge body of research about the uplifting impact a regular gratitude practice has upon mood and your level of happiness. I suggest to my patients that they find a beautiful journal that they dedicate to this purpose and write five things nightly before sleep they feel grateful for.

The third practice that Dr. Arrien identified is to take physical action in the world, such as one that increases the amount of beauty, or to do acts of kindness and charity or to say words to uplift, recognize, and encourage another. In other words, take sacred action.[6] If a person observes these three practices daily—prayer, gratitude, and sacred action—it fosters a feeling of being supported, uplifted, and connected, and it protects against feeling worn down by the

---

6 Angeles Arrien, *The Second Half of Life: Opening the Eight Gates of Wisdom* (Sounds True, 1998).

daily routine, the grim headlines, and the inevitable frustrations and hardships of daily life.

### Ancestor work

In contrast to most cultures around the world, in the United States, there is very little awareness of the importance of honoring the ancestors. Many people know very little about their heritage or their ancestors' stories.

Spiritual practice is enriched by establishing a relationship with the ancestors. This can be done by displaying photos, creating rituals of asking for guidance, and making offerings to honor them. It is my belief that the ancestors are around us all the time and are aware of our lives, of our joys and sorrows. I encourage my patients to talk out loud to their loved ones who have passed and to ask them for assistance.

It is remarkable that family members who occasioned a great deal of suffering and trouble when they were in their bodies can change after death. The relationship with a deceased difficult family member can evolve over time. One of the most talented evidential mediums I worked with is a man from New Jersey named Anthony Mrocka. His accuracy is simply astonishing. He connected with both of my parents by name and relayed messages from them that were deeply comforting. They acknowledged how oppressive it had been for me as a child in our family, and they were both very sorry. They were extremely enthusiastic and supportive of this book project and wanted to know what has taken me so long. A session with a talented medium can have a profoundly healing effect, and I frequently recommend this to my patients.

## Acupuncture points

Another practice that I recommend to my patients is based upon the ancient wisdom tradition of classical Chinese medicine—specifically, the spiritual function and significance of acupuncture points. In traditional Chinese medicine, which is taught in many Western acupuncture schools, as well as in most acupuncture schools in China after Mao's Cultural Revolution, the value of acupuncture was focused primarily upon the physical effects that result from placing needles into acupuncture points while their spiritual significance and function has been split off, disregarded, and even forgotten. Just as in allopathic medicine, in traditional Chinese acupuncture, value is placed upon evidence-based scientific replicability, to imitate and conform to the conventional Western medical paradigm.

This amputation of the spiritual dimension of the points has resulted in a tremendous loss of beauty, richness, meaning, and therapeutic potential. When I have a conversation with a patient about the spiritual dimension of a point that I am recommending to them, it evokes a whole world of associations and emotions that can be harnessed to transform the way a person experiences themselves, their place in the world, and their relationship to their spirit. For example, there is an acupressure point posterior to the angle of the mandible, in the depression on the anterior border of the sternocleidomastoid muscle, called Small Intestine 17. The Chinese name for this point is *Tian Rong*. Needling or massaging this point can have the physical effect of healing tinnitus, sore throat, deafness, and goiter.

The poetic name for this point is *Heavenly Appearance*. It belongs to a group of ten points on the neck called *Windows to the Sky* points. These points are linked to the eyes, ears, mouth, and nose and can support inner clarity. According to acupuncturist, author, and philosopher Lonny Jarret, they are some of the most powerful points for clearing blocks at the spirit level. These points have profound psychospiritual healing power and can be made use of when a person has lost touch with their divine nature, their soul's purpose and calling, and is only aware of their body and personality. Heavenly Appearance is an energy release point that burns away suffering and connects us with the will of heaven. Stimulating this point supports connection of our heart with the heart of heaven and can ameliorate a sense of feeling forsaken by God. How limiting it is to make use of this point only to treat a sore throat! Patients can feel profoundly moved and empowered when given access to a tool like this.

The acupuncture points are energetic centers that, when needled or simply touched, cause a release of energy. According to Chinese medical theory, there are pathways coursing through the body called *meridians* that are like waterways along which energy runs and are associated with various organ systems. Illness in the body, mind, or spirit results when there is blockage in the flow of energy through these pathways. In classical Chinese medicine, there is no distinction made between the body, mind, and spirit. Stimulating the points unblocks the energy and allows it to again flow freely. The points are numbered and named according to the meridian to which they belong, but they also have evocative poetic names that reflect their psychospiritual function. After getting to know a patient, I use my intuition to identify points that they could massage or tap to evoke certain psychospiritual qualities of experience.

Classical Chinese medicine understands health to be contingent upon the balance of five energetic elements or phases—wood, fire, earth, metal, and water—which are all in relationship and mutually either expand or restrict one another. A patient may have an excess or a deficiency of any of the elements, and thus, the aim of the treatment is to rebalance the energetic system. Each element, except for fire, is also linked with two organ systems and their associated meridians, whereas fire is associated with four organ systems and meridians. Emotions are also associated with each element; wood is linked with anger, fire with joy and sorrow, earth with worry, metal with grief, and water with fear. For example, if a patient reports a frequent experience of feeling inexplicably chronically irritable, my intuition might be drawn to an acupressure point on the liver or gallbladder meridian. The liver and gallbladder meridians are linked with the wood element, which is associated with the emotion of anger. If a person is severely suffering for a prolonged period from feelings of loss due to bereavement, I may choose an acupressure point on the lung or intestinal meridian associated with rebalancing the metal element and supporting the metabolism of grief.

## Essential oils

The therapeutic effect of stimulating the acupressure points can be amplified by first applying essential oils to the area. Essential oils are plant extracts made by steaming or pressing parts of the plant—the flower, leaves, roots, seeds, bark, or fruit—to create fragrant volatile chemical compounds. They are essential insofar as they capture the essence of the plant's fragrance. When we inhale, the scent travels quickly through the olfactory nerve to the limbic system of the brain, and it has an emotional effect. Some essential oils are calming, grounding, and nourishing; others are stimulating and energizing—some warming, others cooling. Some essential oils recognized for their antidepressant and anxiolytic effects are lavender, geranium, jasmine, clary sage, bergamot, basil, cedarwood, and frankincense, to name a few.

Essential oils also have metaphysical attributes and effects and have Chinese elemental associations. For instance, citrus essential oils can be helpful in rebalancing the wood element. Essential oils can be used beneficially in combination with acupressure but have therapeutic potential when used in other ways, such as with a diffuser or mixed with a carrier oil and added to the bath, put on the pillow to aid with sleep, or for massage. Some oils should not be applied directly to the skin, so it is always advisable to consult a reliable text, such as Peter Holmes's *Aromatica* series, to determine how to use them safely and to identify reputable sources for purchase. A wonderful book to learn about the sacred aspects of the acupuncture points is *Spiritual Portraits of the Energy Release Points*, by Michele Marie Gervais.

I recommended that my patients order small bottles of these oils, place them on their altar, and massage the prescribed points daily, while contemplating their spiritual meaning. There are hundreds of points and hundreds of oils, and the possibilities are endless for creating rituals to support the mind, body, and spirit in this way.

### *Combining acupressure and essential oils*

Amos is a young man who suffers from autoimmune illness and mold toxicity and who benefited from several of these approaches. When he first came to see me just after graduating from college, his primary symptoms were anxiety, brain fog, crushing fatigue, and diarrhea. At the time, his fatigue was so intense that he had to plan his day around the complete exhaustion he would inevitably experience from the minimal exertion required to just do his laundry.

He was filled with despair because his professional and personal aspirations had been utterly derailed by his illness. He watched his peers progress, as they created the foundation for their futures, getting more education, and establishing love relationships, all of which were completely out of his reach, given his chronic and severe symptoms. He was prone to feelings of shame and lived with the fear of judgment; it was hard for others to understand the disabling nature of his condition. These days, there is more awareness about the challenges of living with chronic mysterious illness due to the prevalence of people with symptoms of long COVID.

Amos is feeling much better now and is taking prerequisite courses to pursue a career in health care. He intends to make use of the knowledge and wisdom gained through the suffering he endured during his own journey with chronic mysterious illness.

In addition to physical treatments for mold toxicity and autoimmune illness, Amos and I have been doing BodyIntuitive energy work, which has included the use of acupressure points. Some of the most frequent points that we have used are these:

### Zu San Li

The point *Zu San Li*, also known as Stomach 36, has the poetic names *Leg Three Miles*, *Lower Tomb*, and *Ghost Evil*. From a physical perspective, stimulating this point, which is located on the lower leg, one hand's breadth below the kneecap and one finger's breadth lateral to the tibia, is deeply nourishing and supports digestion, endurance, and energy levels. (Precision regarding the location is not necessary when massaging or tapping these acupressure points.) On a psychospiritual level, unblocking this energy release point grounds and centers the individual and is a point that supports the manifestation of your gifts and talents in the world. Michele Gervais writes, "It serves to fully integrate the spiritual self and the physical self in order to flow with direct purposeful action of destiny. It strengthens the awareness and realization that there are gifts that only you can bring to the world. That you are an essential part of the plan within the interconnected web of humanity, earth, animal, mineral, and plant kingdom." She goes on to unpack the poetic name *Lower Tomb*: "Sometimes in order to discover one's purpose, one may need to go deep within . . . to draw out and heal painful darkness that one has stuffed in the shadows . . . and discover the buried jewels and treasure. Unblocking this release point strengthens the ability to draw on the wealth of family lineage and wisdom of genetic history in order to resurrect the treasure."[7]

I recommended to Amos that he contemplate the spiritual meaning of this point and its intended physical effects as he massaged this area on his lower legs with frankincense (*Boswellia*) essential oil. Frankincense is made from the resin of trees that grow in the deserts of East Africa and Saudi Arabia. Peter Holmes writes that frankincense essential oil promotes willpower and perseverance and stabilizes the mind and promotes security. It is excellent for discouragement and despair, for mental and emotional burnout, insecurity, and fearfulness.[8] Emily Rowe, MD, a doctor of Chinese medicine and Western medicine in a private communication commented that the Chinese name for frankincense is *Ru Xiang, Fragrance of the Breast*. She stated that it is used to heal nonhealing wounds that are both physical and emotional in nature. One drop of essential oil applied to the points is sufficient. I always recommend that patients apply the oil to the point and then deeply inhale the fragrance from their hands to amplify its effect.

### *Bai Hai*

*Bai Hai*, also known as Governing Vessel 20, has the poetic name *One Hundred Convergences*. This point is located on the crown of the head, the highest point of the entire body, and can be helpful in the treatment of anxiety, headaches, and dizziness. It is thought to lift and calm the spirit and clear the mind, which acts as an antidote to

---

[7] Michele Marie Gervais, *Spiritual Portraits of the Energy Release Points* (Tellwell Talent, 2016), p. 135.

[8] Peter Holmes, *Aromatica: A Clinical Guide to Essential Oil Therapeutics* (Singing Dragon Press, 2019), volume 2, p. 208.

feelings of overwhelm. I recommended that Amos tap on this point while focusing on its psychospiritual meaning. This point is like an antenna that radiates out to the Universe, facilitating the connection between Heaven and Earth, and reminds us of the maxim "As above, so below"; the macrocosm is reflected in the microcosm. The multiplicity of the Universe is contained within the one individual. Unblocking this point creates a feeling of inspiration, creativity, and vitality. It is the point where the energies of Heaven enter the physical body, and thus is an explicit meeting place between spirit and matter. I recommended the use of rose or geranium essential oil on his crown chakra. Rose oil is associated with a heart opening and promotes soothing feelings of unconditional love, comfort, balance, and acceptance.

## Tian Zhu

*Tian Zhu*, also known as Urinary Bladder 10, has the poetic name of *Heavenly Pillar*. This point is located at the top of the trapezius muscle on each side, in the lateral indentation, directly under the occipital bone. Activating this energy release point empowers an individual by connecting them to an inner pillar of strength, allowing them to hold their head high and stand up tall. Gervais indicates that this central spinal pillar of strength connects us to the core of our being and supports faith in ourselves and our clear perception that we have what it takes to complete our work. I instructed Amos to massage these points with frankincense oil and to focus upon aligning with his soul's purpose, thereby increasing his vitality.

There are said to be 361 acupuncture points, each with distinct physical and spiritual qualities and effects, and hundreds of essential oils. The possibilities are endless in terms of creating unique protocols to support a human being in the infinite variety of their experience and need. Lorie Dechar, a visionary alchemical healer, poet, and acupuncturist, has written brilliant, inspiring books that include discussion of the spiritual dimension of the points. One of them, *Kigo*, is exclusively about this topic, and the presentation of the points is organized to harmonize with the seasons.[9]

## Flower essences

In the summer of 2022, I learned to create homemade flower essences during a yearlong alchemical healing mentorship with Dechar and her astrologer husband, Benjamin Fox. I have worked with commercially produced flower essences for years but only recently learned how to prepare them using flowers growing in my environment. Creating them myself is an entirely different experience from purchasing them ready-made and allows for a more immediate and soulful connection to their alchemical power.

Flower essences are diluted healing infusions created from flowers, plants, and trees that can have a profound effect on emotional and physical health and psychospiritual development. They were first created by an English physician, Edward Bach, in the 1930s. Like homeopathic remedies, their mechanism of action is vibrational in nature. They do not affect the biochemistry of the body, but rather, their impact is through the subtle human energy fields, which influence physical, psychological, and spiritual well-being.

The physical process of preparation is as follows: Fresh flowers are collected and then floated on the surface of a glass or crystal bowl of water and placed in sunlight for at least four hours. The warmth and light of the sun diffusing through the petals transfers the energetic imprint of the etheric energy pattern of the blossom onto the water,

---

9 Lorie Dechar, *Kigo: Exploring the Spiritual Essence of Acupuncture Points through the Changing Seasons* (Singing Dragon, 2021).

which then holds the healing archetypal signature of that plant. The blossoms are then removed, the remaining water in the bowl is measured, and an equal amount of brandy is added as a preservative. This is the mother tincture. Five drops of this solution can then be added to a one-ounce bottle filled with three-quarters of water and one-quarter of brandy to create a remedy. Up to seven different essences can be included in a single remedy bottle.

The consciousness brought to the process of preparation is of equal importance. I pay attention to what flower I am drawn to in my garden or what wild-growing flower attracts me. Then I do a bit of research to learn the psychospiritual properties attributed to that flower. If the meaning and effect resonate with me and feel aligned, then I tune into the flower and ask permission to take some of the blossoms to make a healing remedy. After I sense that the flower consents, I harvest a few of the blossoms and express gratitude to the plant. I do the physical process of preparation described with an awareness of communing with a sacred world where magic is woven through everything.

The very first homemade essence I created was from the sweetbay magnolia tree in my garden, the one where I dedicate offerings to the female ancestral line. I associate this tree with my childhood home in Pittsburgh, where a large, beautiful specimen grew beside the driveway. When I had my own home, I purchased one of these trees and planted it in my garden. It blooms in late June and July with waxy, cream-colored, fragrant blossoms. According to the website for the Smithsonian Gardens, the magnolia tree flower is so old that it was alive before the bees appeared, with some fossils identified to be over 95 million years old! The magnolia flower essence supports experiences of profound peace, spiritual fulfilment, and awakening and enhances the capacity to sense the divine in every moment. It dissolves negativity, darkness, and fears, including fear surrounding death. This ancient plant supports the acceptance of divine timing, which is one of the keys to feeling at peace and is foundational to the practice of astrology.

Flowers we are drawn to often contain the precise medicine that is needed at the moment. The next remedy I made was one from a flower named common tansy, which was growing beside the Chestnut Hill Reservoir, where I frequently walk. This flower essence has the property of dissolving procrastination, which I welcomed, as I was struggling to discipline myself to work on this book. The third flower I was drawn to, which was also growing by the reservoir, was evening primrose. This flower essence assists with resolving incarnational trauma, also appropriate for me. As I previously mentioned, my gestation and entry into the world were traumatic, as my mother was profoundly depressed during her pregnancy and suffered from postpartum depression.

The magical phenomenon of synchronicity is evident in terms of which flowers offer themselves to be transformed into healing remedies, which is always astonishing and delightful. Synchronicities function to remind us that, if we listen and are open, the Universe is always whispering to us, sending us guidance and messages. They remind us that we are part of an enchanted world where everything is connected to everything else and provide reassurance that we are on the right path.

As I mentioned, I have used commercially produced flower essences in my practice for years. The qualities of experiences and symptoms that respond to the flower essences are described in a very nuanced manner. This is not a one-size-fits-all pharmaceutical approach that bluntly and generically targets "depression" or "anxiety"; rather, the flower remedies are extremely precise and specific in what they purport to heal. Here are just a few examples:

## Pine

Pine is an essence that many of my patients need. It promotes self-acceptance, forgiveness, and freedom from inappropriate guilt and self-blame. A psychoanalytic framework would understand this as the unconscious guilt remedy. Unconscious guilt causes tremendous suffering and is extremely common. A patient with this problem does not feel as though they deserve happiness or have a right to a life, and they are likely to spoil permissible pleasure, may sabotage themselves, and can make their life a monument to suffering. Along with therapeutic conversation, pine can be a very helpful support in freeing someone from this terrible self-undoing.

## Walnut

Walnut is another of my favorites and is particularly useful during times of transitions, like starting or losing a job, moving, the loss of a partner through death or divorce, starting college, or becoming a parent. It lends courage to follow our own path and destiny and helps free us from limiting influences. It is particularly useful for those people who feel overly constrained by social conventions or familial expectations. Walnut helps the soul to perceive and follow its purpose.

## Scotch broom

Scotch broom is excellent for a particular sort of depression, one that is characterized by pessimism and despair regarding your personal relationship to world events. It is not appropriate for despair that is confined to feelings about your personal life but is, rather, for those who feel overwhelmed by the frightening state of the world. It helps them embrace the vision of a more hopeful and positive world future.

### Red chestnut

Red chestnut is one of the codependence remedies. It helps establish healthy boundaries for those individuals who are overly identified in the role of caretaker and enmeshed in the psychic life of the other. Red chestnut addresses this mental imbalance. It can help to transform negative anxiety and worry about another into healthy compassion and concern.

Since the time of Edward Bach, many new families of remedies have been formulated. The four I discussed recently are from the original repertoire. Often, five or six flower essences are combined to create a unique personalized healing remedy for body, mind, heart, and spirit. These remedies can be a useful and uplifting tool as part of a multimodal healing approach. They can be ingested, applied to acupressure points like essential oils, put in baths, sprayed, or sprinkled on the pillow at night.

## BodyIntuitive and the Heart Chakra Reset

In these transformational times, increased awareness of our hearts and aligning with its wisdom provide courage and compassion for ourselves and others and allow us to navigate our days with balance and equanimity. This is not the heart as understood by Western medicine, a mechanical muscular pump that circulates blood but, rather, the heart as an organ that is a primary locus of consciousness in the body. In Chinese medicine, the heart is viewed as the most central organ and is designated the emperor, the monarch, the supreme controller of the body, mind, and spirit that rules over all the other organ systems, activities, and functions of the organism.

BodyIntuitive is a sophisticated and innovative system of energy healing and medical intuition. The system draws upon both Western medical science and Chinese medicine and was created by a molecular biologist, Laura Stuve, and a Chinese medicine practitioner, Janet Galipo. They invented resets for each of the seven basic chakras that support their health, function, and spiritual power. Chakras are spinning wheels of energy, located in the subtle energetic body, but that also correspond to specific organ systems and nerve plexuses in the physical body. Each of the chakra resets consists of three points, and it is recommended to cycle through massaging or tapping on each of the points three times. The use of an essential oil can potentiate the effect. For the Heart Chakra Reset, rose essential oil, which is very expensive, could be used, or geranium, which is more affordable. Only one small drop of the oil is needed.

Both rose and geranium essential oils calm the limbic system, one of the oldest parts of the brain, a deep structure that regulates emotion, memory, and behavioral responses related to survival. Rose and geranium essential oils support us when we are experiencing the grief of loss, when we feel discouraged or disconnected, or when we are suffering a whole range of distressing emotions such as envy, shame, bitterness, or despair. These essential oils both promote feelings of emotional stability, security, strength, and hope.

Here are the three Heart Chakra Reset points to massage:

### Shen Chu

*Shen Chu*, or Governing Vessel 12, has the poetic name *Sustaining Pillar of Life*. This point is located on the back of the body, on either side of the spine, at the same level as the heart, between the third and fourth thoracic vertebrae, in the area of the upper inside wings of the shoulder blades. Because it may be difficult to physically reach it, focused visualization and imagination are sufficient. Unblocking this energy release point supports the flow of energy throughout the entire organism, assisting in our physical restoration and rejuvenation. It fosters the endurance to persevere and supports our integrity and capacity to speak our truth. It connects us with our energetic roots buried deep in the earth, allowing us to receive nourishment and sustenance while, at the same time, enhancing our sense of being suspended by heaven and our capacity to receive inspiration. It supports our function as a conduit for communication between above and below and empowers our co-creative capacity.

### Shan Zhong

*Shan Zhong*, or Conception Vessel 17, has the poetic name *Center of the Inner Storehouse of Light*. This energy release point can be found on the breastbone, above the heart, located at the center point between the nipples of a man. Stimulation of this point supports the development of our spiritual potential and fosters feelings of peace, joy, and compassion for the self and others. It opens the heart and makes us more capable of giving and receiving love. The activation of this point empowers the capacity to see the divinity in all and to devote ourselves to service to humanity from a place of safety and protection.

### Nei Guan

*Nei Guan*, or Pericardium 6, on the left side, has the poetic name *Inner Frontier Gate* or *Inner Palace Gate*. This point is located two inches distal from the crease of the wrist between the two tendons that run down the center of the forearm. From a physical perspective, it is one of the most well-researched points for the treatment of nausea and vomiting, reflux, and hiccups and as a treatment for morning sickness. Stimulation of this point calms the mind and reduces anxiety. Activation of Pericardium 6 both provides deep access to the heart and functions as a protective point that helps us discern and establish appropriate boundaries with others. The degree to which the heart is held open requires appropriate adjustment according to the circumstances. If the heart is held wide open in an indiscriminate way, we risk overexposure and are vulnerable to being overwhelmed both by our own internal emotions and by the impact of the emotions of others upon us. If the heart is held closed too tightly, we are shut off and disconnected both from others and from the natural world. Stimulation of this energy release point supports the transmutation of pain and suffering in response to experiences of trauma and betrayal into a grateful awareness of the blessings and feelings of peace and calm.

## *The three Ps and meditation*

Ruth King, a Buddhist mindfulness meditation teacher, wrote about the three Ps in the context of bearing suffering.[10] Remembrance of the three Ps provides a very useful and powerful framework that I regularly draw upon in my own life and that I share with my patients when they are suffering. Calling the three Ps to mind is reliably soothing and containing, because they help to bear intense difficult feelings. The Vietnamese monk Thích Nhât Han said that handling our suffering is an art. We can develop skills that allow us to meet our suffering skillfully so that it does not overwhelm us. The three Ps help us to acknowledge, bear, and put suffering into perspective.

The first P is to remember that what happens is not *personal*. When people respond to us positively, negatively, or neutrally, it's because of where they are due to their own conditioning, fear, and suffering. Jack Kornfield, another mindfulness teacher, frequently references the polarity of experiences and emotions that can knock us off a feeling of centeredness, a state of equanimity. Frequently, in dharma talks, he recites these pairs of opposites in a singsong voice, which underlines the

---

10 Ruth King, "The Art of Suffering," RuthKing.net (January 4, 2018), https://ruthking.net/the-art-of-suffering.

daily, repetitive, ubiquitous, and utterly familiar nature of these experiences. Pleasure and pain, gain and loss, praise and blame, prestige and disgrace are all regular features of daily life.

Sometimes, when I publish a blog post, a reader will write to me expressing gratitude and appreciation that I wrote about something that was so meaningful to them. But then the next reader will comment in an extremely hostile and dismissive way in response to the same post. Repeated experiences of this nature have taught me not to become excited and inflated by the praise or deflated by the contempt.

During a potentially upsetting conflict with a loved one, remembering that it is not personal fosters the capacity for compassion when someone behaves in a way that distresses you, which can help you to respond less reactively and more neutrally. This does not mean that you should continue to expose yourself and tolerate it, but it does not affect the way that you feel about yourself or destroy your peace of mind.

The second P is that it's not *permanent*. This is both the good and the bad news. Everything constantly changes. That is the nature of reality. If something is causing suffering, it will pass. It will not last forever. Whatever you love will also not remain the same.

The Five Remembrances are the Buddha's teaching on impermanence, aging, health, change, and death. Thích Nhất Hạn has a lovely version of the Five Remembrances that was part of the liturgy of Plum Village, his spiritual community. He prescribed to his acolytes to meditate upon the Five Remembrances daily to decrease fear and promote acceptance of reality.

> I am of the nature to grow old. There is no way to escape growing old.
>
> I am of the nature to have ill health. There is no way to escape ill health.

I am of the nature to die. There is no way to escape death.

All that is dear to me and everyone I love are of the nature to change. There is no way to escape being separated from them.

My actions are my only true belongings. I cannot escape the consequences of my actions. My actions are the ground upon which I stand.

The recitation of the Five Remembrances is not intended as a depressing litany, from which the only reasonable conclusion that could be drawn is that life is a grim ordeal. To the contrary, the purpose is to encourage us to drink deeply of the present moment, to be fully conscious of our experience, to know that our actions have karmic consequences that we take with us when we die, and to acknowledge that life is inherently hard.

I recommend to all my patients to develop a meditation practice. Meditation grooms and tones the mind and increases our capacity to attend to the present moment. Studies have demonstrated that meditation increases cortical thickness in the hippocampus, the area of the brain responsible for learning and memory, and in other areas of the brain that govern emotional regulation. The amygdala, an area of the brain associated with the fight, flight, and freeze response, decreases in volume with regular meditation practice, which also correlates with the subjective experience of a decrease in levels of stress. The brains of meditators also show fewer age-related changes. Meditation practice has been shown to decrease anxiety and stress, to decrease worry about the past and the future, to decrease depression and rumination, as well as to increase attention and concentration, learning, memory, sleep, attention, happiness, compassion, and empathy.

The third P is that it is not *perfect*. Remembering this can help us bear all manner of disappointment, when things are not the way we would wish them to be or when people act in ways that make us unhappy or angry. It can be helpful to ask myself why I am assuming that it should be different. I think of times when one of my kids is upset with me in a way that does not feel reasonable or warranted. It's helpful to remind myself that relationships are not perfect. Why should they be? Sometimes there are rough patches. It can also be an invaluable tool when dealing with your own perfectionism. When I make a mistake and fall short of my expectations for myself and am ready to blame myself, remembering that I am far from perfect can foster perspective and self-compassion.

## *The power of compassion*

A new book by hospitalist Steve Trzeciak and Anthony Massarelli entitled *Wonder Drug: 7 Scientifically Proven Ways that Serving Others Is the Best Medicine for Yourself* discusses the profoundly uplifting impact that compassion for others has upon our own health, the health of the recipient of compassion, and the health of those who observe the interaction between the giver and the receiver of compassion. Acts of kindness generate joy in the giver, gratitude in the recipient, and emotional elevation in the observer. Compassion is defined as empathy plus action. Acts of altruism stimulate the area of the brain associated with reward and flood the brain with dopamine and endorphins. They upregulate the parasympathetic nervous systems, which calms the fight and flight response. Decreased stress results in less chronic inflammation.

Interestingly, the motivation with which the altruistic act is undertaken counts. If altruism is enacted for personal gain rather than with an intention of true service on behalf of the other, it does not have the same beneficial physiological effect. This is not a transactional practice but, rather, a transformational one.

## *Box breathing and imagining the future*

A breathing technique that I recommend to my patients and do daily during my meditation is an adaptation of a technique described by Lisa Broderick, author of a book about shifting our relationship with time.[11] This technique assists the nervous system to move into a state of heightened parasympathetic tone and relaxation but also supports your capacity to create the emotional experiences that you would like to have. The box breathing technique is practiced as follows:

1. Close your eyes and sit comfortably with your spine straight. Feel the ground under your feet and the crown of your head reaching toward heaven. This posture supports the embodiment of you as a conduit between Heaven and Earth and facilitates the free flow of energy.
2. Inhale slowly through the nose for a count of four.
3. Suspend the breath for a count of four. Exhale slowly for a count of eight. When the length of the exhalation is longer than the inhalation, it is especially calming to the nervous system. As you inhale, imagine your breath as any color that represents what you need at the moment. For instance, imagining blue could have a calming effect, orange could be stimulating, green could be healing, pink could be heart opening. Choose a color that matches what you feel would be helpful. As you exhale, imagine the number three.
4. Suspend your breath again for a count of four.

Repeat steps 2–4 three more times. Each time the sequence is repeated, visualize a lower number. Visualize number two, and repeat

---

11 Lisa Broderick, *All the Time in the World: Learn to Control Your Experience of Time to Live a Life without Limitations* (Sounds True, 2021).

the sequence. Visualize number one, and repeat it again, and then visualize the number zero. When you reach zero, shift your imagination to your future. You can visualize the day that you have planned, or you could envision any wished-for future scenario.

What is important is to imagine how you would like to feel, rather than the specific details or logistics of the events. For instance, I could imagine doing my morning exercise routine and feeling energized and lively, seeing my patients and feeling very present and helpful, FaceTiming with one of my kids and feeling close to them and happy to catch up, having dinner with a friend and enjoying the conversation and meal, then going to bed early, sleeping well, and waking feeling rested. The power of this practice lies in imagining the desired emotional state, which promotes the likelihood of having the wished-for experience. This simple practice is remarkably effective and increases the level of happiness when done regularly.

### *Rose, thorn, bud*

This is a practice that my children and I did together at the dinner table nightly that promotes a feeling of connection and intimacy between people. It is a way to keep up with one another and to know what is on each other's minds and in their hearts. It can also be done with a partner or a friend. Each person takes turns sharing something in their experience that is a rose, a thorn, and a bud. A rose is something a person feels happy or excited about, a thorn is something they are unhappy or angry about, and a bud is something they are looking forward to. When done together on a regular basis, it creates a feeling of warmth and closeness.

## Psychedelic medicines and Internal Family Systems (IFS)

Psychedelic therapies possess tremendous healing powers when skillfully administered in a sacred and ceremonial way and represent a therapeutic breakthrough in the treatment of trauma, addiction, depression, and anxiety. These medicines allow many patients to access much-needed compassion for themselves and others and promote feelings of acceptance and gratitude.

I am very much looking forward to the day when I can offer the full range of psychedelic medicines to my patients without fear of losing my medical license, because they are a uniquely powerful tool for deep psychospiritual growth, healing, and transformation. Currently the only psychedelic medicine that is legal is ketamine. Ketamine has been used very effectively to enhance psychotherapeutic work. It can be particularly powerful when combined with a type of psychotherapeutic approach created by psychologist Dr. Richard Schwarz called Internal Family Systems (IFS). Ketamine can help reclaim what IFS calls the Core Self, who we truly are when all of our sub-personalities, or parts, are integrated. When a person is healed, they have increased access to their Core Self. The Core Self is characterized by the eight C's: confidence, calmness, creativity, clarity, curiosity, courage, compassion, and connectedness, as well as the five P's: presence, patience, perspective, persistence, and playfulness. During these times of accelerated change when people feel so vulnerable, helpless, and fearful, connection with the Core Self fosters resilience, empowerment, and joy.

On a personal note, psychedelic medicines have played an essential role in bringing this book into the world. My journey experiences have enabled me to overcome the belief that neither I nor the book were enough; that if I spoke my truth, my ideas would be ridiculed; and that both the book and I needed somehow to be different. Understanding gained with the use of these medicines helped me to have the courage to authentically share my perspective. Most importantly, I was shown that this is not about me but rather about how I can help at a time of great need when there is so much fear and suffering. For me, as for most people, the impact of developmental trauma has continued to cause suffering throughout the life span, but in the words of the spiritual teacher Ram Das, "We can become connoisseurs of our neuroses," and that can make all the difference!

On a collective level, these medicines enhance awareness of our essential oneness, which may facilitate the shift in consciousness that will promote healing on a planetary level.

## *Community and spiritual friends*

Essential to spiritual development is finding a beloved community of like-minded people with whom you resonate and can feel a sense of belonging and identification. This is not easy. I talk with my patients about local options for this that might resonate. It requires work and effort to create this for yourself. Loneliness is a terrible problem for so many people. Its ubiquity preceded the pandemic, and it undermines any sense of feeling spiritually connected and uplifted. Loneliness often results in a person feeling contracted, small, alone, and fearful. It is so important to have spiritually like-minded friends who share a worldview and who you can communicate your thoughts and feelings with about these matters, share discoveries such as inspiring podcasts or YouTube videos of dharma talks or astrology. It is invaluable to feel supported and accompanied on the spiritual path.

## Developmental psychology and spiritual psychology

We are spiritual beings having a human experience. My increasing feelings of alienation from conventional psychoanalysis is related to its sole focus on the personality self and the developmental history of an individual and its denial of the sacred and the multidimensional aspect of human experience. In my psychoanalytic training, the paradigm frequently emphasized the analysis of a patient's inhibition or conflict around competition, rather than their inhibition to opening the heart to the sacred dimension of experience. The focus was exclusively upon personal history and the ways in which our current unhappiness is a result of the lingering effects of early trauma and pathological attachment styles in the family. There is no acknowledgment of the innate timeless perfection of our nature at a spiritual level. The Zen koan "Each of you is perfect as you are, and each of you could use a little improvement" has nothing in common with the traditional psychoanalytic perspective.

Spiritual bypass can represent a parallel danger, the misuse of spirituality to avoid unresolved emotional issues and to escape the reality of a situation. Some may display a false superiority, a positive toxicity, by which I mean a lack of acceptance of negative feelings, such as anger or sadness, which are characterized as carrying a lower vibration. One woman tolerated an abusive relationship for years because she was afraid to leave. She told herself that she did not take her partner's egregious and cruel behavior personally, that she had risen above it. This was not true, however; rather, it was a means of avoiding taking the terrifying step of leaving him and establishing her independence. Others cling to the belief that their inability to function in the world is the result of a Kundalini awakening rather than post-traumatic confusion and disabling grief, in order to avoid engaging in the painful psychological processing necessary to heal. Given that we are simultaneously human beings who are in physical bodies that are subject to illness, aging, and death and ensouled beings with a spirit that is timeless and nonlocal, we need to integrate both paradigms, both the developmental psychological and spiritual perspectives to heal holistically.

## Cultivating your spiritual life

If you do not currently have a spiritual life that you experience as nourishing, my hope is that you will feel inspired by this discussion to develop practices that support and cultivate the spiritual side of yourself and that you will be enriched and enlivened by doing so. Perhaps you would consider beginning a meditation practice, constructing an altar in the corner of one of your rooms, experimenting with making offerings, practicing the Blessing Way, or learning about the spiritual meanings of the acupuncture points and essential oils to create meaningful, soulful rituals for yourself. Perhaps you would be willing to experiment with oracle cards, crystals, or opening to messages from the Universe via animal encounters. In this way, you will enrich your spiritual connection, add beauty and magic to your life, and elevate your energetic vibration, which, in turn, will have a positive and uplifting impact upon those you interact with. Your very presence will have a healing impact on you personally and the collective planetary consciousness. May it be so!

*Chapter Two*

# THE CURRENT ASTROLOGICAL WEATHER

Let this darkness be a bell tower.
—RAINER MARIA RILKE

An appreciation and understanding of the astrological weather, meaning the planetary cycles and the correlation of those cycles with the archetypal patterns of our lived experiences on Earth, both personally and collectively, can help us to make sense of events at a time when the world around us is undergoing a process of transformation. Astrologer Austin Coppock described it is as though the old world order is undergoing an Etch-A-Sketch erasure process. An understanding of the astrology of these times helps to create a framework for contextualizing the trauma that is affecting each of us and is the context in which the patients who consult me in my holistic practice of psychiatry is embedded. Never in 35 years of private practice have I witnessed events in the external world having such a profound impact on the well-being of my patients and influencing the content of our work together. Even in the aftermath of 9/11, patients had more capacity to compartmentalize and to continue to focus on their personal concerns rather than on collective events.

## Distress on many levels

Initiation is a concept in shamanism where an individual spiritually dies to their old way of being and then comes back to life, reborn and deeply changed. The initiatory experience often involves a catastrophic experience of physical or psychological suffering, and the individual really does not know if they will survive the ordeal. If they do survive, it completely transforms the way that they look at their life. For some people, experiences with psychedelic-assisted psychotherapies are like initiations, in terms of feeling profoundly transformed. A similar phenomenon is observed in those who undergo near-death experiences. Bruce Greyson, a psychiatrist who studies near-death experiences, commented that people who undergo even a few seconds of a near-death experience commonly describe that it can utterly transform their attitudes, values, beliefs, and behavior. People typically become more compassionate, more caring, more altruistic, and much less interested in physical things—in material goods, in power, prestige, fame, and competition.

Current evidence points to a likelihood that a type of planetary near-death experience is what will be required for there to be a collective awakening of humankind that would sufficiently motivate us to collaborate globally to avert environmental catastrophe. As the biosphere collapses at an ever-accelerating rate, the global community shows little indication of coming together to unite in a timely, effective manner to implement measures to avert disaster. It appears that we are entering an initiatory experience, and although many deny on a conscious level that this is the case, the level of fear and grief is mounting in the general population, and people's lives are unfolding against this backdrop of impending disaster.

It is not only the climate catastrophe that is creating intense levels of chronic distress, but political, economic, and social factors are also contributing to increasingly high levels of fear. Belgian psychology professor Mattias Desmet describes the prevailing rational, mechanistic mindset as a closed system that prevents us from resonating with the essence of life. The modern materialist mindset creates a feeling of disconnection from one another and from the natural world and results in a profound sense of alienation and meaninglessness. This sense of dissociation and anomie contributes to an intensifying epidemic of loneliness, which correlates directly with the degree of industrialization and the extent of usage of technology in a country. The epidemic of loneliness was intensified by the pandemic but was already at crisis levels long beforehand. So much so, that in January of 2018, the prime minister of England, Theresa May, appointed a minister of loneliness to address the problem. In a poll prior to the pandemic, 30 percent of people worldwide stated that they did not have one meaningful relationship. In a poll of millennials in the USA in 2019 by YouGov, 22 percent stated that they have zero friends. The powerful impact of social isolation and feelings of loneliness on the body, mind, heart, and spirit cannot be underestimated. It greatly increases the risk of chronic medical illness and dementia, as well as having a markedly adverse impact upon life span.

## Elements and modalities

To appreciate and understand the current astrological weather, it will be necessary to introduce you to some foundational and basic astrological concepts. The four elements in Western astrology describe foundational patterns of energy that manifest as the entire physical and metaphysical world. Understanding and working with these essential patterns is an important and useful part of a holistic approach to healing but also tremendously helpful in making sense of overwhelming and distressing world events. I will begin with a discussion of the elements of Western astrology, because they are vital archetypes that will help provide a framework for understanding what is happening on our planet at this time.

The elements in Western astrology—fire, water, air, and earth—are energetic patterns of consciousness that exist in the world and within each of us in varying proportions. There are also historical epochs that are energetically characterized by one element or another and reflect that quality. The elements are designated by polarity as either feminine or masculine, as either yin or yang, receptive or active. The feminine or yin elements are water and earth, whereas the masculine or yang elements are fire and air. Most individuals have a mixture of yin and yang energies, but this designation does not have to do in any literal way with gender. Each element manifests a different facet of its nature in the three signs of the zodiac belonging to that element.

### THE FOUR ELEMENTS IN WESTERN ASTROLOGY

**The fire signs:** Aries, Leo, and Sagittarius
**The water signs:** Cancer, Scorpio, and Pisces
**The air signs:** Libra, Aquarius, and Gemini
**The earth signs:** Capricorn, Taurus, and Virgo

Fire signs are characterized by action, passion, confidence, and enthusiasm; the water signs by deep sensitivity, the need for emotional involvement with others, empathy and intuition; the air signs by intellectual activity and perspective, detachment and rationality, communication and curiosity; the earth signs by connection with material reality, practicality, building, the physical body, and the five senses.

In addition, the signs of the zodiac are also assigned to one of three modalities, which are linked to the seasons in the northern hemisphere; the cardinal signs initiate the beginning of each season. Aries occurs at the vernal equinox, Cancer at the summer solstice, Libra at the autumnal equinox, and Capricorn at the winter solstice. The fixed signs take place when the season is at its height, and the mutable signs occur when one season is changing into the next. The association of the signs with the beginning, middle, and end of the seasons correlates metaphorically with the qualities of the modalities. When an individual has a predominance of planets in signs associated with cardinality, they are inclined to activity and initiation, and they love to begin projects but may be less likely to follow through. Those with a predominance of fixed signs may be slow to start but, once underway, will be focused and persevering and less likely to change their minds. Those with a predominance of mutable signs are adaptable and attracted to variety and change and sometimes movement and restlessness.

## *THE THREE MODALITIES*

**Cardinal:** Aries, Cancer, Libra, and Capricorn
**Fixed:** Taurus, Leo, Scorpio, and Aquarius
**Mutable:** Gemini, Virgo, Sagittarius, and Pisces

## Applying astrology

Now, with that very brief overview of the elements and modalities, let us see some application. For at least ten years prior to January 2020, astrologers were looking ahead to that time with a mixture of awe and trepidation. They saw an aggregation of planets in the sign of Capricorn, including the meeting of the planets Saturn and Pluto, which signified a time when there would be a global seismic shift. Astrology cannot predict what will happen specifically in terms of events, but it can predict the archetypal weather, and that is what was inspiring alarm. It was clear that something of great magnitude was going to happen that was likely not going to be welcome.

Saturn is closely associated with the sign of Capricorn. It is said to "rule" it. When a planet is in its own sign, like Saturn in Capricorn, it is particularly powerful. Saturn is associated with structure and limits, with time and mortality, and with fear. Capricorn is an earth sign associated with hierarchy, power, governments. Pluto is a planet associated with deep transformation and with repressed, buried shadow material surfacing to consciousness, the exposure of rottenness. One astrologer, Loralee Scaife, commented that when Pluto and Saturn are in relationship in the sky, it's like a pus-filled boil being lanced.[12] Shortly after that, in March of 2020, the global pandemic began, and the world came to a standstill.

On the winter solstice, December 21, 2020, the two largest planets in our solar system, Jupiter and Saturn, met at zero degrees Aquarius, a highly significant event both astrologically and astronomically. Alignments between Jupiter and Saturn occur regularly every

---

12 Scaife is referring to Ptolemeic aspects, the conjunction (0°), the sextile (60°), the square (90°), the trine (120°), and the opposition (180°). These geometrical relationships are particularly significant and denote a combining of the energies in amplifying, supportive, harmonizing, or conflictual ways. In this case, Saturn and Pluto were occupying the same degree, a blending and magnifying of the archetypal energies.

20 years, but this reunion was rare for many reasons. In terms of astronomy, the last time that they were visible in such close proximity to one another was in March of 1226, almost 800 years ago. For ancient astrologers who had no telescopes, Saturn was the most distant planet from the Earth visible with the naked eye. They called the meeting of Jupiter and Saturn every 20 years *the Great Conjunction* and observed that it coincided with major political, social, and generational shifts and upheaval. Jupiter is associated archetypally with expansion and Saturn with contraction. The late, great astrologer Alan Oken called the pair *the cosmic accordion.*

As I mentioned previously, archetypes associated with the planet Saturn are form and structure, time and mortality, fear and limits, realism and practicality, repression and control, discipline, responsibility, and duty. Archetypes associated with Jupiter are faith and optimism, philosophy, law, justice and spirituality, abundance and excess, and blessings.

Some say that the star of Bethlehem was a phenomenon created by a meeting of Jupiter and Saturn, which, according to the nativity story in the New Testament, heralded the birth of Christ. Just as BC and AD demarcated a turning point, a before and an after, I believe that this bright and powerful rendezvous of Jupiter and Saturn was also a threshold moment for humanity. BC could now also come to mean "before COVID," since the pandemic has irrevocably changed our world. Individuals who experience a discrete trauma, such as an assault or any sudden painful loss, often describe feeling that everything in life was different before the shattering event. There is a before and an after. As a nation, we felt a version of this after 9/11, and after the experience of living through the years of the Trump presidency culminating in the assault on the Capitol on January 6, 2021, and the subsequent refusal of many Republicans to acknowledge the reality of what happened and to bring those responsible to justice. The stunning hijacking of the judicial system by a radically conservative Christian majority in the Supreme Court represented another break with reality as we knew it and catapulted us into a disorienting and dizzying new social context.

For the past 200 years, Jupiter and Saturn have been meeting every 20 years in zodiac signs associated with the earth element: Taurus, Virgo, and Capricorn. For the next 200 years, these two planets will meet in signs associated with the air element: Gemini, Libra, and Aquarius. Thus, their meeting on the solstice at zero degrees Aquarius marked the end of one long cycle and the beginning of a new cycle, characterized by very different archetypal qualities and themes. We are witnessing the hard labor as a new world struggles to be born, while we are simultaneously in the midst of a dying process. The world as we knew it is disappearing.

When Jupiter and Saturn mutate from one element to another, this has historically coincided with profound sociocultural shifts. In the 1970s, futurist and author Alvin Toffler wrote a book entitled *Future Shock*. His premise was that the world was changing so rapidly that people could not keep up and felt disoriented by the rate of change. Future shock is prominent now and will only intensify in the next two decades as Jupiter and Saturn journey through the sign of Aquarius. Aquarius is, in fact, the sign associated with the future and a new world order, with technology and innovation, with collective humanity and social groups, with revolution and nonconformity and with dystopia, by which I mean a futuristic social order characterized by oppressive societal control maintained through corporate, bureaucratic, technological, moral, or totalitarian means.

The national and global polarization we are witnessing is, in part, a function of this shift from earth to air. In Western astrology, the element of earth is associated with material tangible things, physical resources, and the physical body. Earth represents the customary measurable three-dimensional time and space reality of separated localized objects that behave in accordance with Newtonian physics. The earth element is linked with what can be known with the five senses—that is, reality that can be seen, heard, touched, tasted, smelled, weighed, and measured. By contrast, the air element is associated with communication, information, thought, analysis, synthesis, and perspective. Air connects everything and has no boundaries.

## From Earth to air medicine

The current conventional Western medical paradigm is a product of the earth element mindset, with its mechanistic approach to the body as matter without consciousness to be manipulated with pharmaceuticals and procedures. The body is not thought to possess intelligence and its own innate capacity for healing. There is no awareness or appreciation of the existence of an energetic body that accompanies the physical body and that has a major influence upon our state of health and illness. The physical body exists in space and ages in linear time, while the energetic body is nonlocal and exists outside of linear time.

Conventional allopathic physicians often specialize in the treatment of just one organ system, not even the whole physical body. There are cardiologists, ophthalmologists, dermatologists, psychiatrists, and so forth, rather than broadly trained practitioners who consider the whole person embedded in a context that includes everything, including the heavens. Holistic healing resonates with the element of air and a quantum physics model, which is not localizable. In the air paradigm, everything, including consciousness, is interconnected and mysteriously affects everything else, and there is no separation in time and space. Our consciousness has been flavored by the archetypal qualities of the earth element for the past 200 years, but now we are experiencing a shift to consciousness that is characterized archetypally by the element of air. People are increasingly opening to the possibility of learning and knowing through intuition and other energetic means, rather than relying solely on the five senses and measurable data.

The materialist mindset that has held sway over the past two centuries while Saturn and Jupiter met in earth signs was characterized by an extractive way of relating to the Earth as inert matter devoid of consciousness. This approach is demonstrably no longer viable, and we are witnessing its devastating consequences in the sixth mass extinction and the collapse of the biosphere.[13] The mindset that has permitted and fostered this way of relating to our world is one of scientific materialism, the idea that only physical reality, as measurable by the natural sciences, truly exists. A belief in the existence of an ensouled world full of divine consciousness is considered primitive and superstitious.

## Astrological cycles

Astrological cycles do not occur in isolation. Cycles often overlap with one another, and sometimes, one cycle reinforces the archetypal meaning of another cycle with which it coincides.

This is the case with the cycle of Jupiter and Saturn, which have met in earth signs for the past 200 years and are now meeting in air signs,

---

[13] Scientists define a mass extinction as occurring when three-quarters of all species die out over a short geological time, defined as less than 2.8 million years. There have been five previous extinction events we are aware of, and none of these others was caused by human activity, or over such a short period of time. The causes of some of the previous extinction events are not entirely clear, but they involved global temperature changes that adversely affected life in the oceans and glaciation that resulted in a loss of habitat, lower sea levels, and destroyed food chains. Other extinction events have been caused by volcanic eruptions. The most recent extinction event was 65 million years ago, when an asteroid eight miles wide struck the Yucatan Peninsula, hurling debris into the air that blocked the sunlight, resulting in a cooling climate and the extinction of the dinosaurs.

with a second shorter cycle of 45 years that is currently both accentuating and echoing the archetypal significations of these two planets.

This second cycle is a square relationship between the planets Saturn and Uranus, which was in effect during the entire year of 2021. This highly charged square between these two planets continued to exert a very prominent influence throughout 2022 and will continue to do so in the coming years. Squares in astrology signify an aspect of conflict and tension, and the squares between Uranus and Saturn often expose cracks in the foundation of our social, political, and financial structures. The essential archetypal meaning of Saturn in this context is authority, the old hierarchy, stability and structure, rigidity, preserving the traditional way things have always been done. The Saturnian energy is in conflict with Uranus, which archetypally signifies freedom and liberation, innovation and the future, rebellion, and revolution, and the totally sudden and unexpected.

The murder of George Floyd in late May of 2021 occasioned a collective awakening to systemic racial oppression and injustice in the USA in a way that felt new. The grotesque evidence of abuse of power by authorities (Saturn) who had been charged and entrusted with the duty to protect was writ so loud and large that it awakened an awareness in those who were formerly in denial of the extent of the racism and injustice of our current system. It occasioned months of demonstrations and protests (Uranus) and a shift in consciousness that cannot be reversed.

We are living through a time in the USA when the dominant group in power, the representatives of the patriarchy, are threatened by the growing population numbers of nonwhite individuals, as well as by the increasing empowerment of women. Saturn is the archetype linked with the patriarchy, a societal structure of male supremacy and oppression that operates at the expense of women.

Historically, when a minority group in power is threatened,

they behave in increasingly cruel, oppressive, dominating, and hateful ways. This is evident in the rulings of the conservative Supreme Court, which struck down the reproductive rights of women in a clear attempt to preserve the power and dominance of men over women, to limit women's freedom and autonomy (Uranus), to control women's sexuality and the process of pregnancy and birth itself. Since that ruling, I have received calls from women who feel panicked by these events, who feel like the familiar world as they knew it is changing in a way that is most distressing. Sovereignty over their bodies, which had been taken for granted, was suddenly revoked.

## Pluto in Capricorn and Aquarius

In 2022, the planet Pluto moved through the late degrees of Capricorn. When the Declaration of Independence was signed, on July 4, 1776, Pluto was at 27 degrees of Capricorn. As I mentioned previously, when a planet returns to the position it was originally at the birth of an individual or where it was located at the inception of an event, the archetypal signification of that planet becomes very pronounced. Pluto was discovered in 1930, and two years later, the capacity to split the atom was discovered. This technology made possible the atomic bombs dropped on Hiroshima and Nagasaki and created the conditions for humankind to destroy itself. This is quintessential to the archetypal energies associated with this planet. Pluto is associated with powerful primal forces. When it is prominent, themes of death and rebirth, of creative destruction, of empowerment and powerlessness, of intensity and woundedness, and of repressed and disavowed material will be dredged up from the depths of the unconscious and experienced by the individual or the collective.

The Pluto return is correlated with increased acknowledgment of the brutal realities related to the birth of the Unites States that have been covered up and allowed to fester, designated by astrologer Jessica Murray as our "original sins." The relatively recent wider acceptance and reckoning with the reality that this country was founded on the atrocity of slavery and on the genocide of the First Nations peoples living here are very consistent with the Plutonic work of owning the ugly truth about the history of the establishment of this country. Cherished self-serving myths can no longer be sustained in the light of the facts.

Pluto in the birth chart of the USA is in the sign of Capricorn, representing hierarchy, entrenched social structures, and the patriarchy. As Pluto travels through the late degrees of this sign, what is rotten about this system is being exposed, and everything that has outlived its usefulness is crumbling as the representatives of the patriarchy struggle to retain their domination and to preserve the status quo.

In March of 2023, Pluto began its move into the sign of Aquarius, where it will ultimately remain for the next 20 years, signifying another shift in consciousness and heralding a major sea change and a very different type of archetypal energy. Pluto's shift from the earth sign Capricorn to the air sign Aquarius reinforces the theme of movement from earth to air. The last time that Pluto was in Aquarius was between 1778 and 1798, the period of the American and French revolutions. The sign of Aquarius is associated with equality, an emphasis on the needs of the collective over those of the individual, the future, higher consciousness, and technological advance. The evolved Aquarian archetype is profoundly humanitarian. Even though Aquarius is associated with the group, it can paradoxically also be linked with nonconformity and progressive, outside-the-box thinking.

An example is that numerous people now dare to openly identify as gender nonbinary. It was previously unimaginable that this would be embraced in such a widespread way. For the many who grew up with a conception of gender as a rigid binary, everyone either male or female, this development is confusing, disorienting, and deeply threatening, as it undermines foundational assumptions. The fact that conceptions of gender have changed so quickly and radically in the last decade is a reminder of what we can expect in the coming years regarding our immutable assumptions. Everything is up for transformation.

The shadow energy of Pluto in Aquarius is characterized by cold rationality and a lack of emotion. It can signify the mounting risk that our lack of wisdom regarding the ethical and safe use of technological advances will result in an increasingly oppressive totalitarian society. Artificial intelligence used for the purposes of surveillance and facial recognition could result in an even greater lack of privacy, as well as the possibility of increased autocratic social and political control, resulting in a profoundly dystopian society. AI will change the way we live more fundamentally than the introduction of the personal computer or the smartphone and can be used for good or evil purposes. If the past is the best predictor of the future, we will find ourselves in even more trouble, given our historical lack of capacity to fully appreciate the unforeseen consequences of technological advance. Our immaturity regarding the wise use of the technology we create bears the stamp of classic Greek tragedy, where our hubris has the potential to be at the heart of our self-destruction.

## Through the birth canal

It can be anticipated that, between now and 2026, the intensity, rate of change, and stress will only increase. All three of the transpersonal planets, Pluto, Neptune, and Uranus, will change signs of the zodiac in a short period of time, which is highly unusual. This coincidence of planetary movement into new signs signifies that the rate of change that we have been experiencing since 2008 will continue to intensify and accelerate. The world as we knew it is disappearing, and it is unlikely that those who have historically benefited from the gross inequity will give up their power without a struggle. The cosmic weather offers support for a course correction or a choice to dig ourselves in deeper. Either we embrace a shift of consciousness and make the changes that enable us to live in harmony and balance with nature or we continue to hurl ourselves headlong into climate catastrophe and technological dystopia.

Many people are understandably in a constant traumatized state of fearful arousal due to the stress of what we are experiencing. When people feel afraid, they are not their best selves. They are more vulnerable to feeling reactive and angry, are preoccupied with personal safety and survival, and have less capacity for compassion, insight, cooperation, and altruism. Having an appreciation of the astrological forces at play can be very helpful as we try to make sense of rapidly changing conditions. These times demand that we become as resilient as possible to meet this initiatory moment that is so full of crisis and possibility with as much equanimity as possible. In my work with my patients, an understanding of the natal chart and the current astrological weather can provide a helpful context to make sense of these times and how each of us is personally impacted.

*Chapter Three*

# THE VALUE OF ASTROLOGY

*A physician without knowledge of astrology
has no right to call himself a physician.*

—HIPPOCRATES

Now that I have given you a brief introduction to astrology and provided an overview of the current astrological weather, I would like to help you understand how astrology can be invaluable for understanding ourselves and others and why it is so meaningful to me. A modern, in-depth understanding of a person from an astrological perspective is a much more individualized, complex, layered, and sophisticated analysis than the Sun-sign-based astrology that is typically found in newspapers or magazines. It can provide both psychological and spiritual insight. The natal horoscope is a symbolic map of our psyche, a sacred blueprint for the evolution of our soul. An understanding of this map provides insight that allows us to better make use of our strengths, to compensate for our vulnerabilities, and it contains essential messages and guidance about life purpose and direction, making it an unparalleled tool for spiritual development.

There are many different schools of astrological thought. I identify as an evolutionary astrologer, which means that I see the horoscope as a sacred blueprint, a map of the evolution of the soul that is growing from lifetime to lifetime. The symbols in the horoscope represent archetypal energies and invitations. As author and astrologer Steven Forrest put it, "Human beings interact creatively and unpredictably with their birth charts." The way that we choose to manifest and express the symbolic energy is related to our level of consciousness and awareness.

How can the cycles and positions of the planets be mirrored by events on Earth? There is an unmistakable archetypal correspondence between events in the heavens and on Earth. I have never come across a persuasive explanation of the mechanics of why this is so. When viewed from the perspective of our cultural conditioning, it makes absolutely no sense. It is indeed a great mystery, but for me, the correlations are indisputable. This correlation contributes to my experience of the cosmos as magical and enchanted and reinforces my belief that the prevailing paradigm of scientific materialism offers a very limited and partial understanding of the nature of our Universe. Astrology is a doorway into mystery of the Universe, or as the gifted astrologer Emily Trinkaus put it, "the study of astrology as an apprenticeship to mystery."

Have you ever stopped to consider how totally astonishing it is that the Sun and the Moon appear to be the same size in the sky, although their diameters are dramatically different? The Moon is 400 times smaller than the Sun, but the Sun is 400 times farther away from the Earth than the Moon, so they appear to be the same size. The odds against this occurring by chance are enormous, and I do not believe that their symmetry is just a random, extremely improbable fluke. In my mind, it is due to synchronicity, a meaningful but inexplicable coincidence with spiritual significance, and it is evidence that we are in relationship with a cosmos that is magically structured and ordered.

The astrological horoscope represents our natal potential, not who we are in a static or fixed way. It is not fated but, rather, illuminates our choices and can empower us through increasing our conscious awareness of the heavenly energies prevailing at the moment of birth. It puts us in a better position to harness these forces and to flow with them, rather than to waste opportunities or struggle against cosmic headwinds. Through this awareness, personal freedom and choice are enhanced. It enables us to become conscious of our true potential and the ways in which we may be needlessly limiting ourselves. It can also be useful in terms of making sense of those periods in life when we experience a confluence of losses or trauma and to identify the astrological correlates, which not only can help put events into perspective but can also provide a time frame for when the difficult weather is likely to pass.

Astrology has helped me to better understand the people in my life, my children, my friends, my patients. When you understand a person's astrological makeup, it fosters compassion and understanding about who they are; the way they think; what, who, and how they love; what they fear; their strengths and vulnerabilities, vocational proclivities, and spiritual nature; and what they are meant to do in this lifetime in terms of their heavenly mandate. It helps us appreciate a person for who they are, promotes acceptance, and mitigates against judgment. It promotes radical acceptance of the self and others.

## Astrological work with patients

In my work with patients, the astrological chart can help identify and integrate all parts of the self, including those that have been disavowed, rejected, and repressed, enabling a person to feel more whole and more fully themselves. For instance, a person may have a natal chart that is loaded with planets in signs that symbolize creative potential, but the person may not think of themselves as particularly creative. Awareness of this potential in the birth chart can be empowering and liberating. A person may have a chart that shows great leadership capacity, public visibility, and power, but they are completely unconscious of that aspect of their potential. Identifying those archetypal symbols can give them permission and encouragement to explore that aspect of themselves.

The following is a description of the work with one of my patients, which will illustrate some of the ways in which astrology can be helpful.

### Transits of Pluto and Chiron

Garland is a lively, attractive woman in her late 40s, the only child of wealthy Jewish parents, who had seen me several times over the years for astrological consultation. Her life was regularly full of intensity and drama. Five years ago, at the time of our last astrology reading, Pluto occupied the same degree as her Capricorn Sun, archetypally signifying experiences of death, rebirth, and total restructuring of her sense of self. At that time, she was in the process of leaving her second husband. Life with him had become so unbearable that she suffered from constant severe abdominal pain, necessitating repeated visits to the emergency room. I recall saying, "It's no surprise that you are coming for a reading now, with so much going on in your chart." This is often the case when someone contacts an astrologer. A person feels in desperate need of help to make sense of an experience of emotional, spiritual, or physical crisis, related to the impact of the current astrological weather upon sensitive points in their natal chart.

I had not seen or heard from Garland for some time when she contacted me during the first summer of the pandemic, asking to schedule a therapy appointment with me, which she had never done before. The following is a bizarre tale of the abuse and misuse of this sacred practice and the astrologer–client relationship.

Garland related that her astrologer, Lisa Ann, who she had been working closely with for four years, was no longer willing to have further contact with her. Lisa Ann had abruptly severed their relationship, stating that she could not help her, after Garland confessed that she had been seeing a man for some time and had been keeping it a secret from her. Lisa Ann was adamant that Garland needed to overcome her obsessive addictive relationships with men and had taken the position that it was imperative that she be single for the sake of her personal growth and development. Garland was emotionally unable to tolerate being alone but did not want to lose Lisa Ann and had thus felt compelled to keep the relationship hidden. When Lisa Ann learned that Garland had gone behind her back, she abruptly cut off all contact with her.

Garland was devastated and frantic, because she had become completely emotionally dependent on Lisa Ann. They had habitually emailed and texted multiple times a day, as well as spending long hours talking on the phone. After four years, Garland had amassed literally thousands of emails from Lisa Ann. Garland had abdicated all sovereignty and had completely handed over responsibility for every decision to Lisa Ann, who would solemnly rationalize her recommendations and pronouncements based upon the astrology of Garland's chart, many of which, when Garland described them to me, made very little sense. She had opinions and judgments about every aspect of Garland's life and issued numerous directives, most of which Garland blindly followed.

Lisa Ann instructed Garland to renounce her affluent lifestyle in favor of a much more modest one and to find honest work in a coffee shop. She counseled her to sever all ties with her friends, who, she maintained, did not really like Garland at all, despite acting as though they did. She also advised her to cut off all ties with her parents, aunts, and cousin. Lisa Ann's recommendations effectively served to isolate Garland from all her other relationships and supports, which magnified her dependence upon Lisa Ann.

Astrologers, like therapists, should not tell their clients what to do. Not only is it unethical, but it is also not realistically within a therapist's or astrologer's capacity to know what another person should do. As I mentioned previously, astrological archetypes can and do manifest in multiple ways, so an astrologer can only illuminate the available potential energies and the way that they impact the client's chart, not predict what will specifically happen.

Lisa Ann was convinced, for reasons that were never clear to me, that Garland's father had a secret life and another family and insisted that Garland do a 23andMe test, to determine whether her father had other children. Garland obediently did the genetic testing and learned, to her surprise, that she was not 100 percent Jewish as she had believed all her life but, rather, that she was half Irish and that her biological father had been a sperm donor. When she tried to talk with her parents about her discovery, her mother insisted that she was crazy and was making all of it up. The man she had grown up with and considered her father told her to "go to hell." There was absolutely no willingness to acknowledge the truth about her parentage or to have any meaningful conversation about it. Reality was utterly denied, which left her emotionally alone with all of it—a familiar experience for her in her family.

Garland began intensive psychospiritual work with me to address wounds from childhood, to heal her terror of aloneness, which was at the heart of her obsessive need for relationships with men, and to make sense of her vulnerability to falling under Lisa Ann's spell, which had translated into an abdication of all responsibility for making her own decisions. She began to reconnect with old friends, who did, in fact, really care about her and who easily forgave her abandonment of them and gladly welcomed her back into their lives. She applied and was accepted to an MFA program, was awarded a generous scholarship, and set to work writing a dark, comedic novel in the genre of magical realism.

She continues to pursue one relationship after another with men, but it has a less compulsive quality and is done much more consciously. She has begun to develop more capacity to tolerate being on her own and to recognize that these liaisons often do not feel particularly nourishing or leave her feeling loved or cherished. Her capacity to tolerate grief has increased. In the past, when she experienced intolerably sad feelings, she would tell bizarre stories that were meant to be darkly humorous but that did not seem funny at all. Instead, I would find myself feeling profound grief and distress as I listened to her. Increasingly, she is allowing herself to be more in touch with her true feelings and to express how much loss she feels about the fact that the man that she grew up with and had always considered to be her father was not biologically related to her. Her ability to acknowledge this to herself represents a breakthrough.

This is the way that therapy often works. Disavowal is a psychological defense mechanism where we know the facts about a situation but are not in touch with the feelings. In this case, Garland had been recently made aware that the man she thought was her father was not actually biologically related to her, but her true feelings about that fact were split off from consciousness and were unavailable to her. She is beginning to allow herself to experience the grief associated with that fact. Hollywood often portrays therapy as a process in which the patient has an experience of scales falling from their eyes as a crucial forgotten traumatic memory is retrieved that finally makes sense of everything. Therapy does not usually work that way. Instead, a person, over time, develops enough emotional strength and resilience that disavowal is no longer psychically necessary, allowing the person to connect the facts with the feelings. This is an important component of the process that is permitting Garland to inhabit herself more fully and to feel in less desperate need of a man to help her regulate her feelings and to ward off the panic engendered by being single.

Astrology has helped us to frame and make sense of her experience. In many of our conversations we contextualize and normalize the intensity and difficulty of her current situation through the lens of Pluto contacting her IC, the *Imum Coeli*, the angle at the bottom of the chart, signifying the deepest most private root part of the self. The IC is the area in the chart associated with the deep unconscious, the family, and the ancestors. The timing of the dark secret coming to light about her parentage is a literal expression characteristic of Pluto contacting her IC. Pluto touching the nadir of the horoscope is fueling the profound psychological work and transformative process we are engaged in. She is ripping up the foundational bedrock ideas about who she is in order to build a new sense of herself.

Pluto is a very slow-moving planet, and the archetypal themes associated with it can endure for a period of four or five years. It's like a slow-moving hurricane that is made even more powerful because it lingers, providing an opportunity to drop lots of rain. When Pluto contacts a sensitive and powerful point in the chart like the IC, there are invariably major changes and upheaval in a life, as well as huge opportunities for accelerated growth, development, and personal and spiritual evolution. Garland has been working to process at a very deep level the impact that growing up in her family has had upon her. Instead of living unconsciously, she is beginning to acknowledge, bear, and put the trajectory of her life into perspective for the very first time. This will likely free up energy to fulfill her heavenly mandate as she becomes increasingly aware and able to bear her feelings.

Simultaneous with Pluto contacting her IC, Garland is also experiencing her Chiron return. The period of the Chiron return at the age of 49 or 50 exerts a psychospiritual developmental pressure to rework essential core issues of woundedness. Garland's natal Chiron is in the sign of Aries, the sign of the self, the "I am," the right to a life and to having your own agenda, personal desires, and wishes. When expressed in an evolved way, it's appropriate selfishness, honoring the true legitimate needs of the self. Garland had never previously given much thought to what she really wanted, why she was here, what she was meant to do with her life. She did not take herself seriously, had no voice, and did not value herself. She was conditioned in her family to serve and to mirror the other, to be what they needed her to be. In keeping with patriarchal values, she had absorbed her parents' projection upon her as being worthy only on the basis of her sexual appeal. She was not in any way accustomed to believing that her thoughts and feelings mattered or had value or that she had a contribution to make or a role to play other than as daughter, girlfriend, wife, or mother.

She briefly vowed to delete the dating apps and to wait until her Pluto and Chiron transits were complete to think about finding a partner. This decision was experienced briefly as an enormous relief and provided psychic space for her to focus upon self-care, her writing and other creative projects, and developing friendships rather than endlessly obsessing about whether a man likes her. She recognized how much of her life force was leaking away as she obsessively texted and rendezvoused with men she had little in common with. Within less than a month, however, she was back on the dating apps, feeling excitement about a fresh prospect and her pleasure and pride in her new freedom were forgotten. There is still psychospiritual work to do to free her from this compulsion, which has historically ultimately been a source of anguish.

Garland and I share a passion for the tarot, and she frequently discusses the cards that she has drawn and what they mean to her. The tarot is a divination tool, an oracle deck of 78 cards, with a particular defined structure. There are 22 major arcana and 56 minor arcana. The major arcana symbolize big karmic spiritual themes and life lessons, whereas the minor arcana are associated with ordinary situations in our daily lives. Within the minor arcana are 16 court cards that symbolize different types of people and character traits and personalities. Each card depicts imagery and symbolism associated with its unique archetypal meaning, signification, and story.

The word *divination* means "conversation with the divine." A premise underlying the use of the tarot for divination is that the cards that are pulled are not random. A question is formulated, and then cards are blindly selected, which are responses to the inquiry. The assumption is that mysterious and meaningful synchronicities are at work and that the cards that are drawn contain the specific message that is meant for the querent to hear at that point in time. There are infinite possible types of readings using different numbers of cards, with varying designated meanings of their positions and questions that can be posed. I do not see the cards as predictive; rather, they are thought provoking and may inspire a different way of looking at an issue. This is not to say that they are merely a tool for developing psychological insight but, rather, that they are a channel through which the Universe communicates with us and allows us to tap into our inner wisdom and knowing, which connects us with the sacred. Regular use of oracle cards such as the tarot promotes the intuitive faculties.

Recently, Garland pulled the tower card again and again over the course of a month. When the same card keeps reappearing at a frequency that defies all statistical probability, there is a need to take special notice, because the Universe is sending an insistent message, trying to get your attention. In this case, the repeated appearance of the tower card mirrors the tremendous process of transformation that Garland is undergoing. This is a time of upheaval, of profound change. She is just beginning to leave her old, limiting, self-denigrating way of being in the world behind and is feeling ready to begin to honor herself and invest in her potential to make a meaningful difference in the world. Her worth is no longer just about her capacity to attract a man. Rather, she is able to ask herself how she is feeling. What is on her mind? Where does she stand? What does she want to communicate with her writing? How can she contribute?

Garland has been studying the tarot for several years with a mentor and recently has begun to do card readings for friends and family. She is very intuitive, and the people she reads for are invariably moved by the experience and find her readings helpful, which feels deeply meaningful to her. She is using herself, her talents, and capacities in completely new ways. Recently, she has been feeling like she would enjoy working with people to help them navigate their lives and has considered training to become a life coach, where she could incorporate her love of astrology and the tarot into her coaching work. She is beginning to feel like she has something of value to offer as a healer and is taking herself seriously for the first time in her life.

Angeles Arrien, the late, brilliant cultural anthropologist who wrote a book of interpretations of the Thoth tarot deck, has this to say about the tower card: "This process is one of restructuring old artificial and outgrown forms of self in order to heal, renovate, and restore that which is actual and true within our nature . . . the process of renovating yourself so that you feel that your outer expression is in alignment with your internal nature. Externally, you begin to dismantle that which is false to fact or outmoded in your life. You shed things, people, and situations in order to restore what is true within your essential nature."[14] The message of the tower card mirrors the opportunity provided by the developmental process of the Chiron return, a homecoming to the essential self and healing of the core wound that estranges us from our heavenly mandate. Garland is coming home to herself and, in so doing, is beginning to offer her unique and considerable gifts to the world.

## Children and astrology

Astrology has helped me to understand my children and to accept and appreciate them for who they are. It does not make sense to expect a tiger to act like a rabbit or a turtle. Each creature has its own nature and entelechy. I have learned the most about astrology and the archetypes through an understanding of my children's charts. These insights have also reinforced my conviction that we are not living in a random Universe; the astrology of their birth charts correlates so clearly with what sort of people they are; their personalities, preferences, and habits; and their strengths and vulnerabilities. When they are struggling, I can see the way in which the current astrological weather impacts their natal charts and can also anticipate when it can be expected to pass. My eldest is a son (he/him), who is 27; my middle child is a daughter (they/them) who is 25; and my youngest is a son (he/him), who is 22.

### *My eldest: Sagittarius and Capricorn*

Although my elder son has a Sagittarius Sun, he has an abundance of planets in Capricorn, an archetype that in the context of capitalism

---

14 Angeles Arrien, *Tarot Handbook* (Putnam, 1997).

and the patriarchy, is conventionally concerned with worldly success, which in this culture is most often associated with making money. The less mature version of the archetype of Capricorn can be quite conservative and conforming, is keenly aware of the opinion of others, and is concerned with social standing. Capricorn is an earth sign, which is linked with the tangible, with resources, manifestation, and the bottom line. It is ruled by Saturn, a planet associated with time and maturity, with limits, security, and fear.

As a junior in high school, my eldest founded a handyman and landscaping company with a friend. The business employed multiple classmates and was profitable, and when they graduated, they sold it to an underclassman. This type of entrepreneurial spirit and functioning as a CEO is characteristic of the Capricorn archetype. His Sagittarius Sun, close to Jupiter, the largest planet in the solar system, magnifies the archetypal symbolism of all that it touches. The proximity between his Sun and Jupiter amplifies his Sagittarian nature. In the kids' high school, there was a tradition of nominating seniors for superlatives—for instance, "most likely to succeed," "most likely to get married first," "most likely to become president," and so forth. My two elder children both had the dubious distinction of being nominated "biggest party animal." They both have powerful Sagittarian signatures, which is often correlated with extroversion and loving a good time. Jupiter is also another name for Zeus, the king of the gods. My elder son has a Leo Moon, which is also associated with the energy of royalty, and confers upon him tremendous warmth, playfulness, great charm and generosity.

The fun-loving, prone-to-excess Sagittarian energy in his chart stands in contrast to his Capricorn energy, which is much more sober and associated with leadership, ambition, hard work, responsibility, reliability, and measurable results. Often, there are very different voices in the birth chart that express themselves, and although they are contradictory, they are nevertheless all true. In college, he only took classes where the grading would be "objective," where he could be guaranteed an A if he answered all the questions right, in contrast to the subjectivity inherent in the way a professor might grade an essay or term paper.

He works in finance, is richly compensated, and for the most part does not voice concerns related to the unfolding planetary crisis. This is not because he is unaware or does not care, but rather because he has difficulty tolerating helpless feelings and talking about sad things. Instead, he regularly donates generously to philanthropic causes, some of which have been recommended to him by his activist sister. He works 15-hour days and does little else during the week except for strenuously working out daily. The need to move and sweat is often characteristic of Sagittarius, but his rigorous discipline is associated with Capricorn.

His fiancée is a lovely, levelheaded woman, from a close and stable family, who works as a nurse. They have been together since their junior year of college and seem well suited to each other. When he was 16, he introduced me to his first girlfriend, who was also a solid citizen. After I met her for the first time, he asked me, "So what did you think of her, Mom?"

I responded, "She seemed very nice, very wholesome." He replied, "Mom! What do I want with a girl who is not wholesome? Why would I want to invite trouble into my life?"

Good question, but not what you would expect from a 16-year-old. His response, however, is very consistent with the archetype of Capricorn, where nothing edgy or unconventional is attractive. Already, at the age of 27, he owns a condo, is engaged to be married, primarily socializes with other professionally successful couples, and has a lifestyle that I associate with someone much older. Those with pronounced Capricorn signatures are often mature beyond their years.

He is so different from me in terms of coloring within the lines and having so little interest or affinity for the magical or sacred. Daniel Giamario, a founder of the Shamanic Astrology Mystery School, has an alternative archetypal association with Capricorn: the Council of the Thirteen Indigenous Grandmothers. He suggests an archetype for Capricorn of thirteen wise female elders who gather to discuss the future and consider the impact of any decision in terms of its effect upon seven future generations. Given that my son has so many planets in Capricorn, which is ruled by Saturn, I could imagine that his Saturn return will be an important turning point for him. It is a major turning point for everyone, but as he has such a concentration of energy in Capricorn, I imagine that it will be particularly impactful. I am wondering and hoping that, at some point in his life, he will begin to embody the archetype suggested by Daniel Giamario. When he was a little boy, he had a passion for all animals, and his ambition was to save the rainforest.

The Saturn return occurs when a person is between 29 and 30 years old and marks the time in which the planet Saturn has completed one full orbit around the Sun and has returned to the natal position in the birth chart. It is a time when developmental pressure is often experienced in terms of setting oneself up for the middle years of life. Saturn is about time and maturity, and the first Saturn return signifies the end of childhood. There is both a social pressure and an internal pressure when an individual reaches that age to have figured out something more definitive about professional direction and personal life. It is a time of getting clearer on one's priorities. People often think about marriage at that time or possibly entertain ideas about starting a family. In this culture, it is not uncommon for someone in their mid-20s to still be searching and finding their way, but by the age of 29, there is more expectation that an individual has a clearer notion of where they are headed. If a person does not feel satisfied with what they are doing or with the direction their life has taken, it is a time when there is often internal pressure to make a course correction.

In my son's case, the personal and professional pieces are solidly in place, but his Saturn is in the sign of Pisces, a sign associated with spirituality and multidimensional experience beyond the five senses. I wonder if something might transpire at that time in his life that will shift his materialist orientation. The most common representation of Capricorn is the mountain goat, who sure-footedly makes his way up the mountain, jumping from one craggy rock outcropping to another. But there is an ancient image of a mythical creature associated with Capricorn, the sea goat, who has a goat body and a fish tail. The sea goat denotes a fusion of the grounded, practical nature that is more commonly associated with Capricorn, with a nature that is much more mystical and creative. I know that the fish tail is an important currently unexpressed part of my son.

Saturn is associated with the father. He is the only one of the three children who has not done a significant amount of therapeutic work to address the extreme trauma that occurred in the family prior to my separation from their father when he was nine years old. His father did not tolerate his vulnerable fish tail nature and humiliated him when he showed feelings, so much so that the sensitive, imaginative side of his nature has become deeply buried. It reinforced his need for predictability, safety, and security, all quintessential Capricornian concerns. I am hoping that his Saturn return will catalyze a reclamation of his birthright and that he will become more comfortable with expressing all parts of himself.

### My middle child: Sagittarius and Aquarius

My second child is a daughter who is 25 and has an abundance of Sagittarian and Aquarian energy in their chart. They live in New

York City, identify as queer, and use they/them pronouns. They are extremely extroverted, fiery, fierce, restless, and iconoclastic. During the lockdown phase of the pandemic, they suffered greatly at the curtailment of opportunity to meet new people, their favorite thing. They love friendship, novelty, learning, adventure, parties, travel, spirituality, and are an ardent social justice warrior and work in the field of sustainability consulting. They frequently change the color of their hair, have piercings and multiple tattoos, love clothes and fashion, and have an incredible artist's eye. They rarely buy anything new, as they are so conscious about the environmental and social justice implications of consumerism, including the sourcing of the raw materials and the conditions of the workers in the countries where garments are manufactured. Instead, they frequent thrift stores and choose eccentric items that I would never have chosen but look striking and interesting when they create an ensemble.

One of the archetypal themes of Sagittarius is a passionate love of truth. In college, they tattooed the word *TRUTH* on their inner lower lip. They are definitive about many things. To be utterly convinced is very Sagittarian, which, of course, has its upside and its downside. It can be overwhelming to disagree with them, as they are so passionate about what they believe and how they see things. They come on strong, which, at times, is challenging for me, as I have a Libra Sun and love peace and harmony and find conflict and debate stressful.

It is interesting to note that they were not always like this. In fact, in nursery school, the teachers made a special point of letting me know that they did not stand up for themselves and were sometimes dominated by other children. They have a Cancer Moon, which confers an extremely sensitive and self-protective nature. Until the age of sixteen, often the sign of a child's Moon is much more evident and overtly expressed than the sign of their Sun. They seemed so much more Cancerian until junior high, when they became much more assertive, and their Sagittarius Sun began to shine more brightly. I was utterly astonished at the eighth-grade parent–teacher conference, when their English teacher clearly did not like them at all and complained that they would not stop talking with their friends during class, despite repeated admonishments. Prior to this, their teachers uniformly simply adored them, as they were not only so kind and eager to please but also extraordinarily creative and intellectually gifted.

Their temperament is very different from mine. I am an introvert, quiet, low-key, and somewhat reserved in a group setting. They are loud and zany and laugh more than anyone I know. At the family dinner table, they would make so many wacky jokes and talk so much crazy nonsense, all the while laughing their head off, that I found it distressing and would sometimes protest that they were giving me indigestion. Their laughter and energy are very characteristic both of an abundance of the element of fire in Chinese medicine and of the sign of Sagittarius, which is a fire sign.

My two sons have the planet Uranus in a position at the very highest point of their birth charts, close to the midheaven. The late famous astrologer Donna Cunningham designated this placement as "You ain't the boss of me." My daughter also has a strong Uranian signature, with multiple planets in Aquarius, which, in addition to all of their Sagittarian energy, also correlates with strong convictions about their own opinions. It's been enormously helpful to know this about my children. As a parent, knowing my children's birth charts helps me to take their behavior much less personally. It's so useful to remember that they each have their own sacred map and that, at some level, their behavior is not about our relationship. There is no reason to take their behavior personally, because they are their own people, with their own birth charts and destinies.

In fifth grade, my daughter was outraged and distraught when they learned about Christopher Columbus and his cruel and violent treatment of indigenous people. They absolutely hated him. In their sophomore year of high school, when all students were required to give a five-minute speech on a topic of their choosing, they spoke passionately about their belief that Columbus Day should be changed to Indigenous Peoples Day and circulated a petition to that effect among the students. Last year, 13 years after their petition, our town of Newton, Massachusetts, officially changed the name of the holiday to Indigenous Peoples Day.

In contrast to their older brother, they are regularly drawn to people who often have very complicated families, much more like their own, where there has been trauma, drama, and dysfunction. They have been in therapy since their sophomore year of high school and are psychologically aware of themselves and insightful about others, although at times, they can nevertheless be breathtakingly self-righteous and intolerant, in true Sagittarian fashion. Their lifestyle is very Aquarian. They share a tiny apartment in Queens with three other queer young people, and on Saturdays, they volunteer assisting in the distribution of organic produce that is offered on a sliding scale, making it more affordable for low-income people.

## *My youngest: Cancer, Cancer, and more Cancer*

My younger son has five planets in Cancer and is a person of tremendous depth and sensitivity, which is characteristic of this archetypal signature. He looks like a romantic poet from the late eighteenth century, with beautiful, long, thick, dark wavy hair, and is as introverted as his sister is extroverted. The archetype of Cancer is very attuned to emotions, the inner life, and personal preferences. It is impossible to oblige someone with a strong Cancer signature to do anything that is not within their comfort zone, that does not feel authentic. They never do anything until they are ready. To attempt to oblige them to do so is futile and doomed to failure. As a parent, understanding that they are late bloomers can be enormously helpful and reassuring. My younger son always hated school with a passion, and it was challenging to get him to do any homework that he did not enjoy or thought made sense. In college, when he could finally choose what he wished to study, he began to blossom.

He recently graduated with a degree in philosophy from a tiny liberal arts college known for providing the opportunity for deep personal connections with professors. Understanding your child's nature with the help of their birth chart can be so very helpful in guiding them in making choices like where they would be happy in college. With so many placements in the sign of Cancer, he would have been lost in the shuffle of a big university. He thrived in an environment where he could establish meaningful relationships and be himself.

He is in love with a woman with whom he has been best friends since junior high. It is very characteristic of someone with so much Cancerian energy to partner with someone who they have known since childhood, someone utterly familiar and safe, and where there is such a depth of connection and history. He just graduated from college at the end of 2022 and is now applying for graduate studies and wants to be a professor of philosophy. After graduation, he moved in with his beloved and is blissful, as he loves domestic life, nesting, and having a delicious meal awaiting his girlfriend when she returns from work. This is all quintessentially characteristic of the archetype of Cancer.

Cancers are very attuned to nurturing and being nurtured, the love of food, cooking, and eating. All my kids love food, but for my youngest, it is his central motivating passion. He watches YouTube videos to learn special cooking techniques, follows chefs on social media, listens to podcasts about ingredients and cooking, and has become a very skilled chef in his own right. He is very close to his family, girlfriend, and professors but, otherwise, does not cast a wide net in terms of close relationships. This used to worry me, but it is clearly what makes him happy.

An analysis of the placement of Mars in the birth chart provides understanding and acceptance of what drives a person and their desire nature. My two older children both have Mars in Capricorn, which is a very powerful and driven placement for Mars and one that pursues its desires for recognition in a direct and uninhibited manner. My own Mars is in Pisces, which has a very different flavor. Mars in Pisces follows intuition, is spiritually and creatively driven, is less goal-directed and more likely to follow the signs and synchronicities or to respond to what the sea tosses up on the shore, and follows the breadcrumbs, rather than making a long-range strategic plan. My younger son also has Mars in a water sign, Cancer, the sign of the crab, which moves by scuttling sideways rather than moving straight ahead. Mars in Cancer is highly sensitive and intuitive and is motivated by what feels nurturing, familiar, and secure. Mars in Cancer does not go for it like Mars in Capricorn and, instead, can be very indirect and self-protective.

Our culture values Mars in Capricorn, an earth sign, with its drive for achievement and material success, much more than the aims of Mars in watery Pisces or Cancer, with its focus upon nurture, sensitivity, and spirituality. My two older children both found internships in the summers between years of college to build their resumes, to improve their chances of getting a good job after graduation. My younger son had absolutely no interest in doing that, which worried his siblings to no end. It was hard for them to accept that he was so different from them. They were both concerned about how he was going to survive in the world. It can be difficult for both men and women, because those archetypes are not in accord with what is most valued culturally. This is particularly true for men, because it is not congruent with the traditional masculine role in our culture and with getting ahead. This is changing, but the great sensitivity, passivity, and indirectness of Mars in Cancer or Pisces have traditionally been considered qualities associated with the feminine.

Understanding the archetypal energies associated with their birth charts helps me to accept and appreciate my children for who they are. I have close relationships with all of them and do not try to change them. Fighting their natures is not a winning strategy. An understanding of astrology supports the blessing of radical acceptance.

## Getting started with astrology

My hope is that this introduction to the potential of astrology to help you understand yourself and the people that you love has intrigued you and will inspire you to get more curious about your own astrological chart. You could buy an introductory astrology text, like the wonderful book written by activist Chani Nichols, *You Were Born for This: Astrology for Radical Self-Acceptance*, or Steven Forrest's classic *The Inner Sky*, or you could consider getting a reading with a professional astrologer. For those who love astrology and are awed by the mystery of its power to make sense of our lives and events in the world, it can become a constant and valued companion. You too can develop a relationship with the stars that will be an endless source of wisdom and nourishment for you and the people you love.

*Chapter Four*

## FOOD IS MEDICINE

> No disease that can be treated by diet
> should be treated with any other means.
>
> —MAIMONIDES

Foundational to a holistic approach to healing is diet. It profoundly affects the way a person feels and their mood, focus, and energy levels, and it can often impact sleep. Dietary habits directly translate into the degree of inflammation in the body, meaning that a diet high in inflammatory foods is usually linked to the development of chronic illness and fuels pain conditions. Given this reality, it's truly astonishing that the entire medical education for doctors typically includes only a few hours of lectures about nutrition. In contrast, there are whole courses devoted to treating illness with medications. There is no acknowledgment of the powerful effect diet has on both preventing and treating illness—particularly upon symptoms that are categorized as psychiatric, such as depression and anxiety.

Margaret Mead, the brilliant anthropologist, wrote, "It's easier to change a man's religion than to change his diet." Our relationship to food is so fundamentally embedded in our personal history in the family, our primary bonds, so closely associated with attachment and comfort, that it is profoundly challenging to make changes in a consistent way. It is not easy to change dietary habits because the associations, both conscious and unconscious, run so deep and because our behaviors are so thoroughly conditioned. Using food for purposes other than physical nutrition is the rule, rather than the exception, and that can be a good thing. People connect with one another through sharing meals, holidays are celebrated, and rituals and traditions are maintained.

Many people, however, have an addictive and compulsive relationship with food. Emotional eating in the face of stress and unbearable feelings is extremely common. Over- and undereating, as well as all manner of restrictive diets, are frequent strategies that many people employ to regulate their emotions. It can feel like a terrible deprivation and a huge sacrifice when I recommend to my patients that they need to avoid certain inflammatory foods, even if those foods are demonstrably causing harm.

Although addiction to alcohol can be overcome with proper treatment, and alcohol can then be avoided entirely, someone suffering from addiction to food has no choice but to continue eating. Most of us eat multiple times a day every day. Certain foods are inherently addictive, such as gluten, dairy, and sugar. Gluten and dairy have glucomorphines and casomorphines, which interact with the opioid system in the brain and have a sedative quality, and sugar is a more powerful stimulant of the dopamine reward system of the brain than cocaine. The processed food industry understands this and capitalizes on our vulnerability. Scientific research is funded to determine how to increase the addictive quality of food and to induce us to buy more. One of the most famous advertising tag lines was the 1983 commercial for Lays potato chips that declared, "Betcha can't eat just one!" This catchy phrase reflects how addictive these potato chips are. No one would be satisfied eating just one of them, because they are so salty, crunchy, and delicious.

Making sustained dietary changes requires a great deal of consciousness and motivation, but the reality is that it is essential for healing holistically. In my initial phone conversation with a potential patient before we decide to meet, I have a discussion with them about their diet. Many will say that they have a healthy diet, but this can mean such totally different things to each person that it's necessary to understand what they mean by it. There is so much disagreement about what constitutes a healthy diet. A person may think that their diet is healthy because they are a vegetarian, but they may regularly consume inflammatory foods such as processed and packaged foods, as well as gluten and dairy.

One of the most common responses that I get from patients when I instruct them to avoid dairy is "Don't take away my cheese!" In my experience, cheese is the food to which people are most fervently attached. They are willing to give up almost everything else besides cheese. Cheese is undoubtedly delicious, but the intensity and depth of their passion is startling and noteworthy.

## Committing to a healthy diet

Given the profound impact of diet on well-being, at a minimum, I request that a patient omit gluten, dairy, and alcohol from the diet; minimize sugar; and try as much as possible to eat a whole foods diet, meaning eating primarily foods that they cook at home and that are made from natural ingredients, rather than processed or packaged foods.

A willingness to make dietary changes is a barometer of the potential for our work to be of benefit to the patient over time. It cannot be overstated how much consistent motivation is required for a holistic approach to be successful. It requires a level of engagement and participation very different from receiving a prescription for Prozac and being instructed to "take one in the morning, and I will see you again in three months."

People simply do not realize how fundamentally diet affects us on so many levels. Surprisingly, they do not realize that there is a direct correlation between what they eat, when they eat, how they eat, and how they feel. Many people feel unwell because they overeat or undereat, or they graze all day rather than eating a meal and eat erratically at different times from day to day. The body loves routines and thrives when mealtimes occur at the same times daily. In the ancient medical tradition of India, Ayurveda, there is a recommendation to breakfast like a king, to lunch like a prince, and to eat dinner like a pauper. This is the opposite of what many in our culture do, which is to skip breakfast and eat the largest and heaviest meal at dinner time. Many feel unwell when they eat too much in the evening, which disrupts their sleep. The adverse impact of eating close to bedtime often becomes increasingly pronounced as individuals age. Some are simply unaware that having a glass of wine or a sugary or chocolate dessert in the evening is disrupting their sleep. For many individuals, when they make small changes like eating less for dinner at an earlier hour, omitting alcohol, sugar, and chocolate, they suddenly begin sleeping so much better.

## *Our food choices and digestion*

Others may feel unwell because they eat too many raw foods, which can be quite difficult to digest. There are those who believe that eating a raw foods diet is healthful, because they believe that the raw foods contain live enzymes that are destroyed by the heating process and that eating the foods raw preserves its vitality. Most people find, however, that it is much easier to digest foods that have been cooked. It is not uncommon for people who eat a raw foods diet to experience bloating and abdominal discomfort. The cooking process makes the food more assimilable and the nutrients in the food more available. The body does not have to do all the work of breaking down the food. The process has already been started by the cooking process.

The same is true for taking the time to slow down and chew our food thoroughly. The digestive process begins in the mouth. When we eat very rapidly and swallow our food without chewing it well, we do not avail ourselves of this first important step in the digestive process. Chewing our food well allows the nutrients to be more readily absorbed and can influence hunger levels. Eating more slowly gives the body more time to register satiation. Chewing food well also mitigates bacterial overgrowth. When large clumps of food that have not been chewed well are swallowed, it can cause bacterial overgrowth in the small and large intestines, resulting in a variety of digestive maladies, including indigestion, bloating, gas, cramping, and constipation. As we chew, more digestive enzymes are produced by the parotid and salivary glands, which aids in the process that continues when the food reaches the stomach. The process of chewing also increases the production of hydrochloric acid in the stomach.

Some of my patients like to intermittently fast and confine their eating window to a restricted period daily. This not only supports digestion but can also be helpful for metabolic health and weight management. Jeffrey Bland, the father of functional medicine, opined in a lecture at an integrative medicine conference some years ago that if we do not give our own digestion at least a 12-hour window of rest daily and tell our patients to do the same, we are not doing the single most important, simple thing that we can do to protect our health.

Extended fasts can also be extremely beneficial for increasing insulin sensitivity, resetting the microbiome, and promoting autophagy. A wonderfully accessible book about the health-promoting benefits of fasting is *The Complete Guide to Fasting: Heal Your Body through Intermittent, Alternate-Day, and Extended Fasting* by nephrologist Jason Fung and Jimmy Moore.

## Eating with the seasons

Many people have no awareness of the benefits of eating in accordance with the seasons. Not only is it possible in our culture to eat strawberries in January, but there also is no recognition that eating lighter foods such as salads in the summer and longer-cooked soups and stews in the winter increases a sense of well-being. If you stop and think about it, it makes perfect sense that our bodies react to the weather and that a hearty chicken soup is not appropriate or appetizing during a July heat wave nor are cold salads appealing in the dead of winter.

In ancient medical wisdom traditions, like Ayurveda or classical Chinese medicine, there is a great awareness of the importance of adjusting dietary practices in accordance with the seasons for optimal health. These traditions are much more attuned to the cycles of nature, and their philosophy of healthful nutrition reflects their belief that human beings are integrated and in relationship with the seasons and the natural world. Health is supported when we live in harmony with our environment. Industrial agriculture and our modern lifestyle, which includes not growing our own food and spending most of our time indoors, creates a divorce from the natural cycles and rhythms of the seasons. This situation is reflected in conventional Western dietary practice and nutritional advice, which is identical for January and August.

## Foods that trigger an autoimmune response

Many feel unwell because most of their calories come from simple carbohydrates or because they eat foods that are processed and contain additives and inflammatory ingredients such as highly processed industrial oils made from canola, corn, or soybeans. Some do not realize that they are having an autoimmune reaction to a food they thought was healthy, such as eggs or corn or tomatoes, and that this food is causing anxiety, insomnia, or joint pain. Eggs, corn, and tomatoes can be healthy foods for some people, but not if you are having an autoimmune reaction to them. This possibility is simply not on their radar, and they are totally amazed when they connect the dots and see the difference that it can make.

## Dilemmas with prescribing diet

There are times when suggesting a change in diet to a patient presents a dilemma. They may have a history of an eating disorder, with restrictive eating and anorexia, and any recommendation to make changes to their diet or to avoid certain foods has traumatic associations attached to it. When someone is too depressed to follow through on recommendations for dietary changes or requests my help in weaning off psychiatric medications but is not interested in making changes to their diet, our work is unlikely to be successful. In such instances, I will not take them on as a patient, because I believe that it will be a waste of their time and money. It's very hard to help someone holistically if their diet is poor.

# Two recommended diets

There are two diets that I routinely recommend to my patients. One is the Paleo Autoimmune Protocol (Paleo AIP), and the other is the

Wahls Protocol. Both are anti-inflammatory diets, but the Paleo AIP is initially more restrictive. The Paleo AIP is an elimination diet that removes all the top allergens, some of which are still included in the Wahls Protocol, such as nuts, seeds, and nightshade vegetables.

## *Paleo Autoimmune Protocol*

If a person has autoimmune conditions, such as Hashimoto's thyroiditis or Graves' disease, or multiple sclerosis, lupus, rheumatoid arthritis, Sjogren's syndrome, or psoriasis, I recommend the Paleo AIP. As I mentioned previously, this is an elimination diet that, in the initial stages, eliminates the top allergens, which include gluten, dairy, eggs, soy, corn, nuts, and seeds; nightshade vegetables, such as potatoes, tomatoes, peppers, and eggplants; and spices like cumin, dill, caraway, and other seed-based spices. All processed and packaged foods and additives are also omitted, as are alcohol, coffee, and sugar. Because it is a paleo diet, all grains and legumes are also omitted.

After the initial phase, which can be 6–12 weeks, the food that a person misses the most can be reintroduced. This is done by eating a small amount of it at breakfast and lunch on two consecutive days and then observing for the next five days. If there is a reaction to the food, which can be increased tiredness, anxiety, depression, pain, headache, worsening symptoms of the autoimmune condition such as rash or other skin manifestation or any digestive symptoms, then the patient must continue to avoid the food. If there is no untoward reaction, it can be safely reintroduced and included as part of the regular diet. The aim is to have the most diverse and varied diet possible of healthy, well-tolerated foods. After the first food has been reintroduced and a determination about it made, a second food can be trialed and so on.

Eileen Laird hosts a website called Phoenix Helix. She is an inspired and devoted woman who has written books about autoimmune resilience and healing. She herself suffers from rheumatoid arthritis, which had been totally debilitating. Through healing with the Paleo AIP diet and lifestyle, she has returned, in her words, "to a full and beautiful life." I always recommend to my patients who are planning to do the Paleo AIP that they purchase her book, *A Simple Guide to the Paleo Autoimmune Protocol*. It is a very slim, accessible volume that contains everything you need to know about how to implement the diet and lifestyle. She also has an excellent podcast by the same name, where she interviews trustworthy guests about all aspects of illness and healing. I recommend to those who are planning to follow the Paleo AIP to listen to the first four episodes, which describe how to implement the protocol and which feature inspiring healing stories.

Some patients prefer to do food sensitivity testing rather than going through the laborious and arduous process of eliminating and reintroducing foods. Unfortunately, my experience is that these tests are not reliable. They seem to both flag foods as problematic that could safely be eaten and to fail to identify foods that should be avoided. I always recommend that my patients with autoimmune conditions do the hard work of the elimination diet rather than the food sensitivity testing. The adage "everything in moderation" does not apply when it comes to identifying food sensitivities. To pinpoint the problematic food, it is necessary to strictly avoid the top allergenic foods during the elimination phase; otherwise, it is impossible to meaningfully assess the response to the reintroductions.

## *Wahls Protocol*

The other diet that I recommend is the Wahls Protocol. Terry Wahls is an internist and clinical professor of medicine in Iowa, a former marathon athlete, and a conventional allopathic practitioner who formerly had little regard for alternative approaches. She was diagnosed with multiple sclerosis in 2000 and, in keeping with her belief system, began to follow all the treatment recommendations for multiple sclerosis, including chemotherapy. This treatment plan did nothing to halt or even slow the course of her illness, and by 2003, her disease had progressed to the point that she needed to use a wheelchair. When it was clear that she was quickly on her way to becoming entirely bedridden, she began to do extensive research, which ultimately resulted in the development of an approach to treating her illness that has diet as the centerpiece. Today, she is again riding her bicycle to work and teaches veterans at the VA hospital to cook.

Dr. Wahls has a cookbook that I recommend to my patients, entitled *The Wahls Protocol Cooking for Life: The Revolutionary Modern Paleo Plan to Treat All Chronic Autoimmune Conditions*. Dr. Wahls has created a food pyramid, which has fruits and vegetables at the bottom. She recommends that a person eat nine cups of fruits and vegetables a day. This sounds like a great deal of produce, but a cup of spinach cooks down to a very small amount. The nine cups of vegetables are divided into three categories, and it is recommended to eat three cups of each. The first group are the greens, which include lettuces, spinach, chard, kale, and all leafy greens. The second category is sulphur-containing vegetables, which are the cruciferous vegetables like broccoli, cauliflower, cabbage, and brussels sprouts, as well as onions and garlic. The third category are brightly colored fruits and vegetables, which means colored all the way through. For example, a carrot or berries are brightly colored because they are one color, whereas an apple is not brightly colored. It is red on the outside and white on the inside. The second tier on the pyramid are allowed animal proteins from responsibly sourced, humanely raised animals;

the third level are nuts and seeds, and the fourth are allowed fats such as ghee, coconut oil, and animal fats rather than vegetable oils.

Dr. Wahls does not permit eggs as part of her protocol. For those individuals who do not have an autoimmune response to eggs, they can be a very healthy food. I recommend that my patients omit eggs for one to two months and then reintroduce them in the manner I described for the Paleo AIP and observe whether or not their body reacts.

## Rage, insomnia, canker sores, and eggs

Ashton is a conscientious woman in her late 20s. She is an accountant, with multiple planets in Virgo, who came to see me because of a fluctuating constellation of symptoms that were causing her significant distress. As is common for people with many planets in Virgo, she had a long-standing interest in holistic health and nutrition that had developed in her efforts to manage a sensitive digestive system. Though not a vegetarian, she was not overly fond of meat or fish and consumed eggs, tofu, nuts, and seeds on a regular basis.

She related that everything in her life was going well. She was engaged to be married to a man she loved, and although her work was extremely stressful during tax season, otherwise it was very manageable, and she liked both her firm and her clients. She tearfully reported that over the past few months since recovering from a gastrointestinal flu, she at least weekly, and usually more often, noted an uncomfortable inner tension mounting inside of her and would feel inexplicably intensely irritable. So far at work she had been able to successfully contain herself, but on more than one occasion, with little provocation she had become enraged at her mother and sister. Her regular angry outbursts were adversely impacting the relationship with her fiancé with whom she lived.

After these episodes, she would feel deeply ashamed and remorseful about her behavior, which left her feeling out of control and as though she did not recognize herself. Often at those times, multiple painful canker sores would appear in her mouth, and she would lie for several hours in bed with racing thoughts before finally being able to fall asleep. The connection between the condition of the gut and our emotions is a reality that is increasingly recognized as a reflection of the health of the microbiome.

I recommended that she take some basic supplements to support her gut health, including pre- and probiotics, as well as glutamine powder to heal her intestinal mucosa, and that she implement an elimination diet, which, not surprisingly, given her Virgoan perfectionism and competence, she did very conscientiously. Soon after omitting the top allergens from her diet, she noticed that the rage episodes stopped entirely. During the reintroduction phase, she discovered that when she ate eggs the angry outbursts and canker sores returned, as well as the insomnia. By avoiding eggs, she was entirely free of all three symptoms.

This is not an uncommon story in my practice. Identifying and omitting trigger foods can make a dramatic difference. Yet despite knowing that this is the case, people will consciously choose to eat the offending food and then suffer the consequences. Ashton knew that eggs caused these symptoms, but on occasion she would decide to have some anyway. At least then she could connect the dots, anticipate the likely emotional and physical responses, and pre-emptively take a sleep medication prior to getting into bed. Making the connection resulted in feeling much more in control of her life.

Sometimes a symptom is only mildly unpleasant and transient, like causing postnasal drip or a headache, and a calculation is made that it feels worth it to indulge on a special occasion—drink a glass of wine, partake of a cheese board or special pizza, or eat later than usual—knowing full well what the consequences will be. As you can see, identifying and getting clear about specific food triggers can empower conscious choices, rather than simply being at the mercy of the body reacting in ways that seem unpredictable. In fact, it only seems random due to ignorance of the causal relationship between a food and a symptom. In many cases, the triggers are totally predictable; they just need to be identified.

## A variety of plant foods

I also recommend to all my patients that they aim to incorporate 30 different types of plant foods into their diet weekly. Every plant food has its own prebiotic fiber profile and feeds a distinct population of microbiota in the gut. The health of the gut is predicated upon the diversity of the microbiome. By eating a wide variety of plant foods, the diversity of the types of microflora is supported. A healthy population of gut flora translates into support for the immune system. Think of our hunter-gatherer ancestors prior to the advent of agriculture, who roamed throughout the countryside gathering a variety of plant foods, upward of 200 different types, each with its own unique phytonutrient profile.

Our modern diets are so very limited regarding the variety of vegetables that we consume regularly. When we try to incorporate 30 different plant foods, herbs and spices can be included in the tally. If a person is conscious of this goal, it's possible to intentionally add a great variety of different vegetables to a salad or soup, which supports the health of the immune system.

## The vitality of food

The vitality of food is not something we are accustomed to considering. In our culture, we talk about calories and the macronutrient profile of foods—how much fat, carbohydrate, and protein it contains—or we talk about its vitamin and mineral content—for example, citrus as high in vitamin C or spinach containing iron. We do not talk about the quantity of qi in food.

Qi is a concept in Chinese philosophy and medicine that refers to the energetic life force. A freshly picked fruit or vegetable is full of qi, and when we eat it, we assimilate its vitality into our body. The more time that has elapsed from when a fruit or vegetable was picked, the less qi it contains. When a zucchini was picked in Mexico several weeks ago, refrigerated, and then flown thousands of miles to end up on the shelves of our supermarkets, a significant amount of time has elapsed. By the time that you purchase that zucchini, leave it sitting in your refrigerator for even more time, the quantity of qi in it has diminished considerably. In contrast, when you buy produce at a farmer's market or participate in a farm share or grow your own food, the freshly picked fruits and vegetables are brimming with vitality.

This contrast is all the starker when you consider a box of cereal, cookies, or crackers. How long ago was the grain the product was made from growing? When we consume processed packaged foods, it provides us with empty calories that are devoid of qi and instead supplies our body with foods that are inflammatory. For many people, most of the food that they consume comes from those sorts of foods. This is particularly true for people with less education about food or with lower incomes who live in food deserts, where there is no fresh produce available. The only items available for purchase are processed and packaged foods, which are usually less expensive. A pint of blueberries may cost five dollars and a box of macaroni and cheese one dollar.

I ask my patients to eat at the same times each day if possible. The body absolutely loves routines and responds with increased well-being when provided with a schedule of regular mealtimes, sleep, and exercise. Healthy digestion is supported by eating substantial meals and avoiding snacking in between. This is contrary to previous conventional nutritional wisdom that advocated grazing all day. The digestive system needs time to rest and recuperate and is supported when it is not obliged to constantly assimilate newly ingested foods. This approach to eating also supports healthy levels of insulin and mitigates against insulin resistance. Insulin is the hormone that helps regulate the levels of blood sugar. Many patients, especially those suffering from anxiety and digestive issues, feel much better when they eat warm, long-cooked foods with plenty of good fats.

It is not only the quantity of qi contained in food that contributes to the power of food to heal and nourish us. When we take time to pause before eating, bless our food, and express gratitude for the miracle of what the Earth provides and to all the beings who were responsible for the food arriving on our plates, we also raise the vibrational healing quality of our food. So many people miss this easy opportunity that we have multiple times daily to connect with the sacred and to express our gratitude. It is also important to create a peaceful, unrushed atmosphere at mealtimes and to avoid stressful, controversial discussions, which also undermines digestion. All these mindful spiritual practices are supportive of nourishing ourselves holistically.

## Organic food

I ask my patients to buy organic foods as much as possible because there are so many toxins and pesticide residues on our foods that degrade our health, harm the microbiome, and thereby create inflammation in the body and brain, not to mention the detrimental impact of conventional agriculture on the environment.

The Environmental Working Group publishes a yearly list of the Clean 15 and the Dirty Dozen.[15] The items on this list change somewhat from year to year. The Clean 15 are those foods that do not have

---

15 https://www.ewg.org/foodnews

high pesticide or toxin residue on them and for which conventional versions can safely be bought. The organic versions are more costly, and choosing the conventional version does not have a significant detrimental impact on health. On the 2022 list of the Clean 15 are avocados, sweet corn, pineapples, onions, papayas, frozen sweet peas, asparagus, honeydew melons, kiwis, cabbage, mushrooms, cantaloupes, mangoes, watermelon, and sweet potatoes. The Dirty Dozen are those fruits and vegetables that have been identified as containing the highest amount of toxins and pesticide residue. Only organic versions of these should be consumed. The Dirty Dozen list includes strawberries, spinach, kale, collard and mustard greens, nectarines, apples, grapes, bell and hot peppers, cherries, peaches, pears, celery, and tomatoes. Strawberries and spinach had the highest residue for six years in a row.

Eating cilantro and beets regularly can support the body in ridding itself of toxins. Beets promote the release of bile from the gallbladder, which binds to fat-soluble toxins to carry them out of the body through our stools and cilantro supports the detoxification of heavy metals.

## Supplements

The following are a few very basic supplements that I routinely recommend to patients: 2,000–5,000 IU of vitamin D with 100 micrograms of vitamin K supports immune and hormonal function, healthy bones, and teeth. Magnesium glycinate at 400 mg twice a day supports multiple organ systems in the body, including nerve, muscle, and bone function and healthy immune and cardiac systems. I impress upon my patients the importance of a daily bowel movement. If constipation is an issue, they can use other forms of magnesium in addition to magnesium glycinate, like magnesium oxide or citrate, both of which have a laxative effect.

If they do not have an issue with histamine intolerance, I often recommend a soil-based probiotic and ask them to regularly include fermented foods in their diets, like sauerkraut, kimchi and other pickled vegetables, nondairy yogurt, and kombucha. Fermented foods are an effective and inexpensive source of natural probiotics that support the health of the gut microbiome.

Taking 1,000 mg of fish oil with both docosahexaenoic acid (DHA) and eicosapentaenoic acid (EPA)—omega-3 fatty acids—daily can support the immune and nervous systems. Attention to quality and freshness are particularly important. This can be obtained in either supplement form or by eating small fatty fish, such as sardines or mackerel. NAC 600 mg twice daily, a precursor of glutathione, supports detoxification. Selenium 200 micrograms, either in supplement form or including two or three selenium-rich Brazil nuts daily in the diet, is very supportive of the thyroid and immune system. Turmeric, between 500 and 2,000 mg daily, is a powerful anti-inflammatory herb to include regularly. Berberine, 1,000–1,500 mg daily, increases insulin sensitivity. If symptoms related to the health of the gut are prominent, I often recommend butyrate to support the lining of the cells of the intestine and glutamine powder to nourish and heal the intestinal mucosa. All of these are very basic generic supplement suggestions that should be supportive of most people. It is important to choose a quality brand of supplement. A few brands that I trust are Thorne, Apex Energetics, and Integrative Therapeutics.

## The psychospiritual function of the continuous glucose monitor

Paying attention to appropriate nourishment for your unique body has a profound impact on the capacity to feel spiritually connected. When the body and brain are inflamed, it lowers the energetic frequency, which results in an experience of contraction, anxiety, and depression. Any kind of loss or trauma can translate into inflammation, and inflammation can darken the mood, increase the level of fear, constrict consciousness of interconnectedness, and diminish the sense of spaciousness. When inflammation in our bodies is kept at low levels, there is more potential to feel uplifted and connected to our intuition and to something greater than ourselves.

Recently, a few of my patients have begun using continuous glucose monitors (CGM) as a wellness tool. None of them are diabetic or prediabetic, but keeping their blood sugar stable and within a healthy range has had a profound effect on their overall mood and well-being, including the level of their depression, anxiety, cognitive clarity, and energy. The improvement is related to a decrease in inflammation. I have been frankly astonished by the changes I have witnessed in these patients in a short period of time.

A CGM is a sensor that is applied to the fatty part of the upper arm and is checked by holding a smartphone, loaded with an app, to the sensor. Individuals check their blood glucose multiple times a day. This device provides feedback in real time about the effect various foods have on their blood sugar levels. The information provided by the CGM serves to increase their awareness and motivates them to eat in such a way that does not spike their blood glucose. Spikes in blood glucose are associated with an inflammatory response. It erodes the denial and dissociation about how daily, moment-to-moment food choices are impacting their well-being.

One woman in her early 50s, with a great deal of Virgo in her chart, was prone to criticizing herself and others. She was often vulnerable to taking things personally and to feeling hurt by interactions with her children and husband, as well as by feeling overwhelmed by simple household tasks. Using the CGM motivated her to change her diet. Now only a couple of short weeks later, she is so much calmer, has much greater perspective, and is approaching her life and her loved ones with a remarkable wisdom and compassion that was previously absent. She also feels very capable of managing and organizing her household.

The anguish and resentment have vanished and have been replaced with equanimity, humor, and competence. This is a psychospiritual transformation related to stabilizing her blood sugar. When we feel physically unwell, access to our higher self is obscured. We are more vulnerable to feelings of shame, guilt, anger, and criticism of ourselves and others, and filled with fear rather than love. The body, mind, emotions, and spirit are all interconnected, and the health of the body is integral to a sense of well-being, resilience, and spiritual connection.

Three simple effective steps can have a major beneficial impact upon insulin sensitivity and blood sugar stability:

1. Take a walk after eating. This causes the skeletal muscles of the body to take up circulating glucose, which moderates blood sugar spikes and reduces the amount of insulin secretion necessary.
2. The order in which types of foods are consumed during the course of a meal makes a big difference. Eating non-starchy vegetables first, good fats and protein second, and leaving starchier foods for last has a significant impact upon increasing blood sugar stability and reducing glucose spikes. For example, eating asparagus and salad first, then salmon, and then rice.
3. Remarkably, ingesting 1–2 tablespoons of vinegar in an eight-ounce glass of water 20 minutes prior to eating also has a powerful capacity to reduce blood sugar spikes after a meal via the slowing of the emptying of the stomach contents. Any type of non-sugary vinegar will do. Apple cider vinegar is always a good choice. It is to be noted that some people with histamine intolerance have an adverse response to vinegar, so as usual, it's important to know the unique response of your own body.

*Chapter Five*

## BREAKING AWAY FROM ENERGY VAMPIRES

When people show you who they are the first time, believe them.
—MAYA ANGELOU

I was honored when my esteemed mentor and colleague Neil Nathan invited me to contribute an essay about energy vampires to his courageous new book, *Energetic Diagnosis*. This chapter will expand on the thoughts that I shared about this topic in his book.

It may come as a surprise to you that your interpersonal relationships foundationally contribute to your physical, emotional, and spiritual health or illness. Please keep an open mind about this because I can assure you that I have met very few patients who are in frequent close contact with a person who is mistreating them who do not suffer health consequences from the stress, anxiety, and depression that this type of relationship causes. It is also an extremely common occurrence that the current abusive relationship represents a repetition of a relational dynamic from the family of origin and thus carries distressing resonances that evoke conscious and unconscious associations. This pattern results in an even more powerful undermining of your well-being, but more about this later in the chapter. Holistic healing cannot occur in this context, and you must avoid contact with the person who is mistreating you. This is unfortunately nonnegotiable if holistic healing is your goal.

Absolutely everything that we experience has the potential to contribute to our growth on a soul level. Spiritually, we become involved in relationships with people who will offer the opportunity for our soul to evolve and to learn the lessons that we are meant to learn in this lifetime. In my own case, I married a deeply traumatized man who was an energy vampire like my father and who provided me with the painful but perfect circumstances to alchemically transform the wounds that I experienced in my family.

When my first child was born, the planet Pluto was at the same degree of the zodiac as my north node, a point in the birth chart that particularly signifies our heavenly mandate. My north node is at zero degrees of Sagittarius, in the first house, signifying that speaking my truth is essential to my life purpose in this incarnation. One of the archetypal significations of Pluto is empowerment. The abusive dynamic in my new family provided me with the opportunity and necessity to stand my ground with my former husband. I felt compelled to defend my son in a way that had been impossible for my own depressed mother, and I did not pass on my experience of betrayal and abandonment to my own children.

I offer this piece of personal history as an illustration of the rich opportunities for soul growth and development in our most heartbreaking and traumatic experiences, including the current predicament that humankind faces during these times of collapse. This perspective is an invaluable lens to view all our challenges and sorrows, because it offers the possibility of transforming terrible suffering into high-octane fuel for our psychospiritual development.

## Toxic relationships

When a new patient consults with me, their symptoms are most often a result of impaired immunity, which is expressed physically as inflammation of the body and the brain. Inflammation can manifest as myriad physical, psychological, and spiritual symptoms and can have a variety of common causes, including autoimmune illness, environmentally acquired illness, infectious illness from microbes, alienation from the spiritual aspect of the patient's life, and psychological stress, to name a few. Patients may seek help because of depression, anxiety, alienation, insomnia, an inability to concentrate, and fatigue, which are all related to inflammation. These psychiatric symptoms are often accompanied by physical symptoms as well, such as digestive and skin symptoms and chronic pain.

If a person is simultaneously involved in an interpersonal relationship that is causing them to suffer, the correct diagnosis, appropriate physical and psychological treatment, and spiritual practice can only help to a limited degree. It is not only toxic relationships with intimate partners that can have this effect; chronic relational stress with a parent, sibling, child, friend, employer, or coworker can also have a similar impact.

A patient can do everything right, meaning that they adhere to the cleanest diet; take a wide variety of precisely chosen, high-quality supplements; include adequate daily movement as part of their regular routine; practice sophisticated sleep hygiene; receive regular bodywork from skilled practitioners; and have a meaningful professional life, loving family relationships, a dedicated spiritual practice, and connections with supportive friends and community, but if they are involved in a toxic relationship that is causing significant distress, it is unlikely that they will be able to really heal without minimizing contact or ending the relationship altogether. A toxic relationship not only causes psychological and spiritual pain but also results in chronic arousal of the sympathetic nervous system, known as the fight, flight, or freeze state, which has an adverse impact upon the immune system and causes cellular inflammation.

## Malignant narcissists

Another name for energy vampires is *malignant narcissists*. These are individuals who take advantage and exploit others and typically do not feel conflict or guilt about doing so. They do not respect the Golden Rule: "Do unto others as you would have others do unto you." The concept of mutuality or relational reciprocity is a foreign one and they feel entitled to constantly take without giving in kind. These people are often shrewd and calculating opportunists, adept at considering every angle to ensure that all interpersonal transactions will work to their advantage. Malignant narcissists can exhibit a range of pathological behaviors, from extreme self-centeredness, irrationality, drama, and volatility to exploitation, frank aggression, and sociopathy.

The field of psychiatry has a diagnostic manual that provides guidelines for the assessment and diagnosis of psychiatric conditions. It features a section on personality disorders, which are a group of conditions that involve a pathological way of thinking, behaving, or relating to other people. Personality disorders are rigid, dysfunctional, long-term patterns of behavior that cause serious problems with love and work. Typically, patients who qualify for a diagnosis of a personality disorder are not aware of the way others are responding to them. Their behavior is egosyntonic, meaning that they are not troubled by their own behavior, and they do not think that they have a problem. The problem is that others are distressed by their conduct.

Psychological help is typically sought because a person feels unhappy. They may have a sense that there is something about the way that they are feeling or thinking, the way that they are relating to others and approaching their life, that is causing them distress. It is often due to a recognition that they keep finding themselves in the same unwelcome situation or repeating a painful relationship dynamic, and they have insight into the fact that they are doing something that is getting in their own way. They recognize that the problem is inside of them.

Malignant narcissists don't look at things that way. It is quite rare for malignant narcissists to seek help from a therapist. If there is a problem, it is the fault of the other. They chronically externalize blame. It's always someone else's fault if anything goes wrong. Sometimes they may appear in a therapist's office under duress: Their partner has given them an ultimatum—either they get treatment or the relationship is over. This is obviously not a situation that is conducive to a successful psychotherapy.

Here is a case study that was included in the essay that I wrote for Dr. Nathan's book. You may think that this sounds implausible, but there are many people who have no concept of mutuality and who are completely self-interested. It is by no means rare. If you are in a relationship with a person like this, it is best to separate from them as soon as you can. That may sound harsh, but, tragically, this is not a condition that I have seen respond to any kind of treatment. It is very sad to give up on someone, but, unfortunately, continuing to try and get a person like this to take responsibility for their behavior and to change is, in my experience, doomed to failure. This may sound extreme and counter to cultural conditioning, particularly for women but often for men as well. We are taught that we should never give up on another person, that unconditional love and persistent dedicated effort will cause the other to change their ways. We can fix them. This is not my experience when the partner is a malignant narcissist. It is simply not possible for people with this type of personality structure to change and to be capable of engaging in the mutual, reciprocal give-and-take of a healthy relationship. I have had many patients who have been partnered with people who fit this description and have never witnessed them being willing or able to change.

From the metaphysical perspective of reincarnation, it is sadly true that if in this lifetime a person is incapable of mutuality, it is possible that in a subsequent reincarnation the quality of their relationships will be very different. They may evolve and become very capable of loving and respectful interpersonal connections. Holding an enlarged, expansive view allows for the possibility of a soul's continued psychospiritual evolution across lifetimes.

## Loni's chronic fatigue

Loni was a 40-year-old woman who came to see me because of severe anxiety, depression, and insomnia. She had been married for seven years to an unscrupulous, wealthy real estate developer 10 years younger than herself. She slavishly served him, anticipating and attending to his every need, trying desperately to get him to respond in a loving, caring way to her, just as she had tried in vain to get her narcissistic mother to acknowledge and be kind to her.

As a result of the relationship dynamics with her husband, she had developed severe chronic pain and fatigue, which was diagnosed as fibromyalgia. Although she enjoyed their lavish lifestyle, she recounted with embarrassment stories about her husband bullying hostesses in restaurants, claiming that they had lost his reservation when he never had one in the first place until they finally capitulated and gave him a table. Once, when he scratched his car in a parking garage, he claimed that it was due to the carelessness of the valet at the restaurant where he subsequently dined and demanded that the restaurant pay for the repair. He threatened to sue his dentist to avoid responsibility for a bill for extensive dental work. Aggressive browbeating and intimidation of others resulted in him almost always getting his way.

My patient became more and more debilitated over the course of her marriage. Finally, when he took up with a much younger woman and announced on Valentine's Day that he wanted a divorce, she was heartbroken. She reported with shock that he had suggested dividing up their possessions there and then. I was hardly surprised. It sounded predictable and consistent with everything that had preceded it.

They divorced, and she moved to the other side of the country to start a new life. When I received a card from her a year later, she related that her depression, anxiety, pain, and fatigue had quickly evaporated once she was free of him. She wrote that she was training for a marathon and felt like a new person. As dramatic as this sounds, it is not an uncommon story, insofar as a toxic relationship can totally undermine a person's health and well-being.[16]

## Getting out from under the energy vampire's spell

When I was in my residency, a supervisor ironically once observed that "a narcissist and a masochist is a marriage made in heaven." He explained that the narcissist thinks that they deserve everything and the masochist thinks that they deserve nothing. I do not like the attribution of masochism to someone who feels undeserving of treatment with love and respect, which has, in my mind, a victim-blaming connotation, but the concept of narcissism is one that is still quite useful, and unfortunately, the condition is very prevalent. Holistic healing cannot occur if one is involved in a relationship with a person who has this type of personality disorder. It creates too much stress, anxiety, and depression.

---

16 Neil Nathan, *Energetic Diagnosis* (Victory Belt, 2022).

Narcissism is a spectrum disorder. On one side, there is the individual who is mildly impaired; they exhibit selfish, self-absorbed, and entitled tendencies. On the other side is the severely disturbed malignant narcissist, who I described previously. This more disturbed type of individual can often be good-looking, charismatic, and confident, and they can present as larger than life. Many very successful individuals in our culture who are drawn to positions of leadership in the government or business have this personality profile.

In a romantic partnership, those with the more severe form of the personality disorder often initially "love bomb" the partner during the courtship. They are charming, attentive, and flattering and are given to grand gestures and are sexually adept. They have an uncanny and frightening intuition about the vulnerabilities of their partners. They know exactly the words to say and what they need to do to cast a spell on their victims to dominate them. The victim is engaged to be of service to them and to provide "narcissistic supplies." If they fail to meet the demands, they are often subject to intense negativity, blame, criticism, and rage.

As I mentioned previously, it is much more common for people who are victims of this type of person to seek help than it is for the narcissist themselves to do so. The partner of the narcissist is often the adult child of a narcissistically disturbed parent. It is a familiar experience to have their basic and appropriate needs for love and respect ignored, their boundaries routinely violated, and their feelings invalidated.

This pattern of relating is profoundly familiar and feels like love and home. When they were children and expressed a need or a feeling, they were criticized and told that they were selfish and much too sensitive. They were praised for being totally devoted to taking care of the needs of the narcissistic parent. Trying to win love through service and sacrifice is all that they have known, and it feels utterly comfortable and normal, although, to any impartial observer, it looks completely mad. It is more the rule than the exception that people repeat patterns of relating that were learned in the family. These can be healthy adaptive patterns or deeply painful and dysfunctional ones. Frequently, an individual partners with someone who they believe is very different from a parent or sibling they had a difficult relationship with, only to eventually reexperience the same painful relationship dynamic.

Freud called this the *repetition compulsion*. The theory is that the person is unconsciously re-creating early traumas in an attempt to gain mastery over it. The hope and wish are that, this time, the situation will turn out differently. Unfortunately, this is rarely the case, and the result is a repetitious retraumatization, made even more painful because it evokes all the sorrow of the original wound.

It is natural and to be expected that patients who are partnered with malignant narcissists feel depressed and anxious and experience insomnia. When they report these symptoms to their primary care physician or seek consultation with a psychiatrist, it is common to recommend that they take antidepressant, antianxiety, or sleep medications. Medications can help them tolerate the stress of being partnered with someone who is critical, manipulative, cruel, and deceptive. Medications can numb a patient so that they are better able to withstand the abuse. When a patient stops these medications, they often can no longer put up with the mistreatment. I sometimes feel like I am engaged in the work of liberation when I help a patient wean from a medication that has had the effect of numbing them to corrosive effects of abuse. The distress engendered by having their own needs systematically ignored and invalidated is the necessary condition for them to consider protecting themselves and getting out of the situation.

If a victim of a malignant narcissist has the futile hope that the relationship can be salvaged and improved and persuades the partner to go to couples therapy, it is vitally important that the couples therapist be aware of the relationship dynamic of the couple. Many in the mental health field do not understand this and ascribe to the adage "It takes two to tango" and treat the couple as though the responsibility for the dysfunction in the relationship is equally shared. They do not recognize that one of the members of the couple is much more damaged and damaging than the other. It is crucial that the therapist not add insult to injury by recommending even more accommodating behavior by the victim. Many couples therapists do not understand this, and this form of couples therapy can make things much worse for the victim. It is unfortunately a common blind spot in the field. Many partners of malignant narcissists harbor a vain hope that the relationship can be worked on, and they keep trying, even though it's futile and doomed to failure. They cannot accept that the relationship cannot be fixed. Only when they finally accept the reality of their partner's limitations will they be able to separate from them and begin to heal.

I have treated patients whose couples therapist recommended that they continually acquiesce to the unreasonable, relentless demands of the narcissistic partner to avoid conflict. They were advised to accept the gross distortions of reality and to agree that white is black and black is white to keep the peace. This advice is destructive and undermining and only further diminishes the poor self-esteem of the victim partner and increases their level of depression.

I witnessed one patient who was determined to try this strategy. She deliberately agreed repeatedly to what she knew to be false and absurd, just to appease and to avoid conflict. This was temporarily workable, so long as the disagreements were between her and her husband. But when his paranoid delusions and distorted accusations began to involve their children, she could no longer go along with the charade and felt compelled to separate from him.

It is not uncommon that, when a narcissist is left, they vow revenge and begin a dedicated campaign to cruelly punish the partner who will no longer submit to them. Frequently, malignant narcissists in these situations recruit the children to participate in their war against the partner who left, sometimes effectively causing parental alienation from the victim parent. I have seen firsthand the terrible emotional damage done to children when the narcissist wages a relentless vendetta against the partner who initiated the separation.

## *Dolores learns to honor her feelings*

The following is another example of a woman whose partnership with a narcissist eroded her health. Like Loni, only when she finally left the narcissist was she able to heal.

Dolores was a social worker in her late 40s who was married to a lawyer considerably older than her. She had been diagnosed 10 years previously with chronic fatigue syndrome and had been prescribed multiple psychiatric medications for depression, anxiety, fatigue, and attentional difficulties, but she had continued to work despite the increasing severity of her symptoms. She was feeling so unwell at the time of our initial consultation that she had just taken a medical leave of absence from her role as a social worker in an agency that served children whose parents suffered with substance abuse and mental illness.

Dolores was the only child of two professionally successful, alcoholic parents. She saw little of her parents during the week because they worked long hours, and she was cared for by a series of housekeepers. On the weekend, her parents regularly started drinking before lunch and, by the evening, were significantly intoxicated. They praised her for being self-sufficient and "mature." This meant that she did not ask them for much and certainly did not express how she was feeling.

Dolores was a good student, had a few friends, never caused trouble or drew much attention to herself in any way, except in terms of her health, which had never been robust. She suffered from frequent headaches and caught whatever virus was circulating. She attended a small liberal arts college and then went on to get a master's in social work. She had always been shy and had never dated much. She met her husband at a fundraiser for her agency; he had been invited because his firm provided pro bono legal services. He was the first man she had a serious relationship with, and they married after a year.

By then, she was in her mid-30s and very much wanted to have children. Although he had two children from a previous marriage, he had assured her that he would love to start a family with her. After a couple of years without conceiving, she eventually initiated a conversation with her husband about getting a medical workup to determine the cause of their infertility. At that point, he disclosed that he had had a vasectomy prior to meeting her. He had not wanted to tell her because he was afraid that she would not marry him and then had continued the deception because he was afraid she would leave him if she found out. Instead of being outraged or expressing feelings of betrayal, she said that she understood how difficult this must have been for him. She did not acknowledge her own feelings of anger and shock but, instead, focused all her empathy on his experience instead of her own feelings.

Shortly after this revelation, her symptoms of chronic fatigue began. She felt tired no matter how many hours of sleep she got, and often felt dizzy. Her headaches became a daily occurrence. She had trouble concentrating and became increasingly depressed and anxious. Trials of one antidepressant and anxiety agent after another, mood stabilizers, and sleep medications, as well as medications to help her focus, were initiated, but none of them helped. She felt so chronically unwell that she gave up on any further conversation about having children with her husband. She did not broach the possibility of adoption or any alternative technology-assisted conception.

When she walked into my office, I was struck by her thinness, pallor, and the dark circles under her eyes. She looked much older than her 49 years. When she related the history of her symptoms of chronic fatigue and linked their onset to the revelation of her husband's deception, I wondered about her seeming lack of outrage at the betrayal. I noted how she portrayed it as so difficult for him. She cared more about his feelings than her own. It took many months of therapy for Dolores to understand that this did not make sense. She had been so thoroughly conditioned since early childhood to care about how other people felt, rather than about her own experience. A childhood history of this type of brainwashing is very common in the partners of malignant narcissists.

This was the most dramatic and consequential example of the dynamic between her and her husband, but there were myriad other smaller examples of the way he disregarded her wishes and preferences. When they went out to eat, he always chose the restaurant. He never asked her where she might like to go, and she never tried to express her wishes. The smell of cigars made her feel nauseous, but he continued to smoke them in the house and car, even though she asked him not to do so and had told him that it made her feel sick.

As she talked about her marriage with me, she very slowly began to recognize her sadness about her life and anger at her husband. She was particularly devastated about not having been able to have children. She asked me for a referral for couples therapy, but he refused to accompany her. She eventually decided that she could no longer stay married to him and left. He tried to exact financial retribution during the divorce process, but she had a good lawyer, and he was not successful. He repeatedly took her to court to try and have the decree altered, but it was upheld.

As soon as she left him, she began to feel better. Her energy levels increased, her spirits rose, the dizziness stopped, and the headaches became much less frequent. We worked on gradually weaning her from all the psychiatric medications that had been prescribed, and she began to focus on taking care of herself in a way that she had never done previously. She started eating a more healthful diet, started walking daily and doing yoga, and made friends with other women at the yoga studio.

When she felt strong enough to go back to work, she left her position at the clinic where she had been working with the children of substance-abusing parents and began to work at an agency that provided services to women who were victims of domestic abuse. She especially loved working with groups and became very skillful at empowering the group members to take their own needs and wishes to heart.

## Breaking free

It is a true blessing when the trauma and suffering resulting from the relationship with a malignant narcissist ultimately results in the spiritual transformation and psychological maturation of the victim. This can only happen when the victim is finally able to truly acknowledge the painful reality of the situation and accept that they do not have the power to change their partner. Only when they no longer agree to engage in this type of destructive one-sided relational contract will they be able to part from the narcissist and to begin the work of healing. In these cases, the victim is finally ready to accept the horror of what they were willing to participate in, and ultimately, their self-respect demands that they no longer endure being treated in a way that they would ever treat anyone. The childhood fantasy of omnipotence is relinquished, and they finally accept that, no matter how sincerely they try, no matter how much they sacrifice and devote themselves, the narcissistic parent will not be transmuted magically into the longed-for caring, loving parent by their efforts. They accept the bitter reality that it is not within their power to persuade the dysfunctional parent to love and care for them appropriately.

In an analogous way, when they finally admit that they will never be able to change the malignant narcissist into a rational, reasonable, and kind partner, family member, friend, or boss, they are freed. Ironically, the acceptance of the limits of their capacities is empowering and paves the way for profound psychospiritual evolution. In this way, a malignant narcissist can be a great spiritual teacher, offering the victim transformative lessons in the blessings inherent in the acknowledgment of reality, providing them the opportunity to be profoundly matured through their grief and suffering, and catalyzing personal growth and self-love.

I hope that it is evident now that this type of imbalanced relationship results in health-destroying stress, fear, and despair in the victim, which can have a far-reaching impact upon every organ system in the body, but particularly the immune, endocrine, and nervous systems. The burden of dealing with a malignant narcissist can put the immune system into a state of chronic overreactivity, which can result in an autoimmune condition, or conversely, it can suppress the immune system, predisposing a person to become particularly vulnerable to infections and toxins. Chronic stress affects the body by causing cellular inflammation. It is exceedingly common for me to see a patient with severely compromised immunity who also reports high levels of stressful, adverse experiences in the present, the past, or both. It is frequently related to childhood trauma but can also be due to states of chronic sympathetic arousal in adulthood. When a patient is regularly victimized by a malignant narcissist, it is essential to the healing process that they become conscious of the reality of the nature of their relationship. This will eventually enable them to make the necessary changes to their situation so that they can free themselves and create the conditions for healing to occur.

## Accelerated resolution therapy

Many patients who have been in abusive relationships develop a post-traumatic syndrome. In my practice, I frequently recommend accelerated resolution therapy (ART), an eye movement therapy, to help metabolize and heal traumatic experiences of all types. ART, originated by Laney Rozenzweig, is an efficient, effective, and creative technique for treating trauma, chronic pain, stress, and a variety of psychiatric conditions, such as phobias, obsessive–compulsive disorder, and depression. It is being used successfully in the military to treat PTSD, but its applications are much broader than for treating only trauma, including some surprising successes in conditions like fibromyalgia.

The beauty and uniqueness of ART rests not only upon how remarkably quickly symptoms are resolved, usually in between one and five sessions, but also upon the prominent role the imagination and metaphor play in the healing process. Practitioners are instructed to carefully adhere to a standardized multistep script that has been precisely and thoughtfully crafted, and the patient follows the directions. The patient is instructed to pay attention to their bodily sensations in between privately imagining scenes. If the sensations are distressing, they are removed, and if they are pleasant or positive, they are amplified. At each step, the patient follows the practitioner's moving hand to stimulate smooth pursuit eye movements, which is one of the elements through which the therapeutic action of ART occurs. Ultimately, the patient visualizes a wished-for scene and outcome. This method of voluntary, positive image replacement is one of the key features that distinguishes ART and is at the heart of the success of the method. Rosenzweig has also drawn upon Gestalt therapy techniques, where a patient might recruit earlier selves or imagine wished-for conversations with relatives as part of the healing process.

A session can usually be completed in 75 minutes. ART uses smooth pursuit eye movements, similar to the rapid eye movements that are present when we dream, which reconsolidate memories. ART is loosely related to eye movement desensitization response (EMDR), in that both make use of eye movements, but they differ in fundamental ways. Rosenzweig has said that ART goes way beyond desensitization and actually "positivizes" memory. The technique uses voluntary replacement imagery generated by the patient to change their affective relationship to memory.

ART is not hypnosis. The brain waves generated by the two methodologies are quite different. A patient does not lose the knowledge of what occurred, but the memory loses its negative adverse charge. One of the unique features of ART is that it is not necessary for the patient to share much of their internal process with the practitioner. There is no need for the patient to tell their story again. The scenes can be played out privately in their own mind. Practitioners are therefore not as likely to experience vicarious traumatization as they accompany and guide the patient and facilitate the process, because they are not exposed to the painful material in the same way as with EMDR or other existing modalities.

Three criteria are essential for ART's success. The patient needs to be able to hold onto thoughts for the duration of the session, needs to be able to move their eyes, and must be motivated. This last caveat is the most complex. My training in psychoanalysis has sensitized me to factors such as unconscious guilt and other conflicts and inhibitions that create resistance to change. I am nevertheless consistently impressed with the efficacy of this deceptively simple technique and continue to recommend it when a person is suffering from the lingering impact of traumatic experiences.

## Energetic practices

There are many different representations of the structure of the chakra system, but one common description is that there are seven basic centers extending from the crown of the head to the tailbone along the midline of the body. They are vortexes of spinning energy that correspond to nerve plexuses and the endocrine centers. Chakras can be visualized as a collapsible vegetable steamer opened to a specific aperture and that faces both front and back. The second chakra is located three fingers below the umbilicus. This is the chakra center from which we engage in emotional relationships with other people and apprehend others' feeling states. Jill Leigh, a gifted energy healer, taught that the aperture of the second chakra should be opened only 20 percent. She said that most people walk around with their second chakra wide open and are thus overwhelmed by the energetic vibration and feelings of others in a way that violates their emotional and psychic boundaries. The only time the aperture should be held wide open like that is when we are surrounded by pristine nature or making love with someone we love; otherwise, it should be set at 20 percent. I recommend that my patients energetically focus upon closing the opening of their second chakra to 20 percent aperture in order to maintain appropriate boundaries and to mitigate against unintentionally absorbing the energy of another person. This practice can be helpful when anticipating a difficult conversation or when an environment feels overstimulating or overwhelming in any way. It's a useful tool to have on hand and can serve many purposes.

Pink yarrow, a flower essence, can be particularly useful for those who are prone to absorbing another person's energy and who are easily influenced by the emotions and actions of others. It can be helpful in setting and maintaining healthy, appropriate boundaries and can protect on both an emotional and a spiritual level. This can be a helpful remedy to call upon when trying to disentangle oneself from a relationship with an energy vampire.

## Reflect upon your relationships

Do you recognize aspects of yourself in the descriptions of Loni or Dolores? Are you in a relationship that is causing you distress and undermining your well-being and self-esteem? Are there ways that dysfunctional dynamics in your family of origin are repeating in your relationships as an adult? If you are in a relationship that is eroding your health and you are suffering from anxiety, depression, or a chronic mysterious illness and systemic inflammation, it will be imperative for you to make the necessary changes to your situation if you wish to feel better. This type of relational pattern is not one that is easy to just shift quickly, but with the right therapeutic relationship and support, over time, it will be possible to empower yourself to feel ready to separate yourself from the relationship and to create the conditions for healing and transformation.

*Chapter Six*

# WEANING FROM MEDICATIONS

> The person who takes medicine must recover twice, once from the disease and once from the medicine.
>
> —WILLIAM OSLER, MD

Many patients who come to see me have been taking medications for anxiety and depression for years and would like to stop taking them. They often do not feel like the medications are really helping them to feel better and have tried to stop them on their own, either cold turkey or over a short period of time. These attempts to discontinue the medications often result in distressing withdrawal symptoms, such as disabling anxiety, depression, mood swings, difficulty concentrating, insomnia, headaches, tiredness, irritability, sweating, unstable blood pressure, racing heart, dizziness, brain zaps (sensations of electrical shocks or jolts), nausea, and even flu-like symptoms, including chills and aching muscles, to name a few.

Some patients report that, when they asked their prescribing psychiatrist or nurse practitioners to help them get off the medicine, some have outright refused, insisting that the patient needs to be on the medication because they will be at risk of a recurrence of symptoms if they discontinue taking them. Prescribers who do agree often lower the dose much too quickly. In my residency training, we were taught to cut the dosage by half and then by another 25 percent and then to simply stop it altogether. This quick decrease in dosage was not considered to be in any way potentially problematic or to put the patient at any risk.

When a patient does experience an increase in symptoms because of this rapid decrease in dosage, these symptoms are often misunderstood and seen as a relapse of the condition for which the medications were prescribed in the first place and as evidence that the patient needs to remain on the medication and not as related to a withdrawal syndrome. A 2019 study in the *Journal of Addictive Behaviors* reported that more than 56 percent of patients who attempt to come off antidepressant medications experience withdrawal symptoms, and half of those characterized their symptoms as severe.[17] Many of the psychiatric medications have intrinsic antihistaminic properties, and when the dosage is decreased quickly, there is a rebound of histamine, which can result in the symptoms that I mentioned previously.

The threshold for prescribing psychiatric medications is very low, and many doctors do not warn their patients about how hard it may be for them to stop taking them. Doctors are not trained to consider or suggest other healthier approaches to addressing anxiety and depression beyond prescribing medications. There is no conversation about psychospiritual or lifestyle factors, including nutrition, movement, time in nature, and alcohol consumption.

In the current conventional medical primary care system, there is

---

[17] James Davies and John Read, "A Systematic Review into the Incidence, Severity, and Duration of Antidepressant Withdrawal Effects: Are Guidelines Evidence-Based?" *Journal of Addictive Behaviors* 97 (2019): 111–121.

no time for this. The average appointment is 15 minutes long, and a patient often does not see a provider who they have seen in the past; the provider does not know them or have an established relationship with them. Clinicians are burned out by the inhumane, soulless conditions under which they must work, including the huge volume of patients that they are required to see, the treatment algorithms that they are obliged to follow that obliterate their agency and creativity, and the massive amounts of documentation required. They often do not have the bandwidth or patience to really listen or connect with their patient. This is a systemic problem and one that is driven largely by the powerful political lobbies of the pharmaceutical companies. Each treatment algorithm concludes with which drug to prescribe. This medical care model is based upon greed and corporate profit and not public health or well-being.

In 2020, 45 million Americans were taking antidepressants, or one in seven. During the pandemic, prescription psychiatric medications increased 21 percent. Antianxiety medications like benzodiazepines are only meant to be taken short term, such as when a person with a phobia of flying must take a plane or to adjust to a time-zone change, because the risk of psychological and physical dependence is very high. If a patient takes benzodiazepines for even a week, they can run the risk of withdrawal symptoms. There are many patients who have taken them for much, much longer, and when they try and go off them, they experience nightmarish discontinuation syndromes. I frequently receive calls from patients whose doctor had been prescribing them high doses of benzodiazepines, then retired, and the patient's care was transferred to another doctor. The new doctor was uncomfortable with the high dosages and wanted them to get them off the medications or at least to take a much lower dose. The new doctor lowered the dosage very quickly, causing a horrific withdrawal syndrome that was extremely traumatizing.

## Taking a holistic approach is a major commitment

When I agree to work with a patient to get off medications, I make it clear that I will be recommending a holistic approach that is not simply about reducing the dosage of the medication. They must agree to taking a multimodal approach, or else I am not the right person to help them with this. Taking a holistic approach to reducing medications is a major commitment. Unfortunately, but also understandably, there are people who assure me that they are ready to do what it takes to wean from medications, and they may have the best intentions, but when they are required to do a daily mind–body practice, to consistently adhere to dietary changes, to spend time outdoors in the sunlight, they are unable to follow through. They are entirely sincere when we spoke but simply do not have the wherewithal to implement the necessary changes.

Sometimes, this is because they are too depressed and have trouble accessing the motivation. Sometimes, their brain fog is too severe to follow a complex daily treatment regimen with multiple steps that involves a regular commitment. I try and anticipate this with prospective patients before we meet, to explore with them the fact that this is a significant undertaking and to let them know that it will be a waste of their time and money if they do not feel like they can follow through on my recommendations. When they prove to be unable, it often seems like they think that they are capable of it but underestimate how hard it will be for them.

I regularly get calls from parents whose teenagers are depressed or anxious or think that they have ADHD. Their child is insisting that they want to see a doctor to get medication, frequently reporting that their friends are all taking them and that they want medication too. Given the nature of my practice, the parents who call me are clearly a self-selected group, and they are often horrified that their child has their heart set on taking pharmaceuticals. They are clear that they do not want their child to just take medications before exploring a more natural approach. If a teenager is not in agreement with taking a holistic approach, this will never work. If they are determined to get a prescription and do not want to make dietary and lifestyle changes, their parents are not going to be able to compel them, and the treatment will be doomed to failure. I do not agree to see teenagers who are insistent about getting medications. I need a collaborative partner to be able to help.

## The importance of context

Initially, it is important to get a comprehensive understanding about what was going on in a patient's life that resulted in the prescription of medications in the first place. It may have been symptoms of depression or anxiety in response to a trauma or loss, such as illness or death of a loved one or a divorce, a postpartum response, or after a medical illness, or a car accident. It may have been in the context of a move to a new home or starting a new job, in which case I am interested in the question of environmental toxicity, particularly mold exposure. It is important to understand what caused them to become so symptomatic in the first place that resulted in receiving a prescription for medications.

In this context, I always want to know about their experience in their family of origin, to better understand the ways in which their stressors may be echoing past trauma. For instance, a move to a new city as an adult may feel quite different to someone who grew up in a military family and was obliged to move every few years in childhood, which created a need to constantly start over establishing new friendships. Or a divorce may trigger painful childhood memories about their parents' acrimonious divorce and the ensuing disruptions and lack of stability. It can be very therapeutic to make these connections more conscious. It can enable the patient to become more aware of the ways they are mistaking the current situation for the past. They are reexperiencing childhood feelings when they were totally overwhelmed by the situation, when they had far fewer coping resources and much less choice than they have now as adults. It can be a game changer to remind them that then is not now and that now they can take care of themselves and reach out for help and are no longer victims of their difficult circumstances.

## The Gupta Program

I almost always recommend that patients who want to wean from psychiatric medications do a self-guided mind–body neurorehabilitative practice called the Gupta Program, which can be downloaded from the internet. This program uses guided meditations, visualizations, mood elevation, simple movements, and trauma-informed techniques, including identifying and interrupting triggers. The program is designed to rehabilitate a part of the brain called the limbic system—specifically, the amygdala and the insula. All limbic-retraining programs are based on the brain's inherent neuroplasticity, its ability to form and reorganize synaptic connections, especially in response to learning or experience, or following injury.

The limbic system is a collection of deep structures in the brain that relate to both individual and collective survival functions, like reproduction, caring for our young, and our emotional and physiological response to danger. It operates outside of our conscious control and is integral to processing emotions, memories, and arousal. The insula controls autonomic function through the regulation of the sympathetic and parasympathetic systems and has a role in regulating the immune system.

When the limbic system gets stuck in a hypervigilant reactive mode, it can misperceive situations that are either neutral or safe and respond to them as if they were dangerous. The sympathetic nervous system, which controls the fight, flight, and freeze response, gets activated when a person experiences danger, either consciously or unconsciously, even when there is no real danger.

The parasympathetic nervous system is responsible for the relaxation of the organism and promotes the functions of rest and digestion. *Digest* is usually used in reference to the process of digesting food, but I believe the meaning of this verb can also be usefully expanded to include processing and digesting all sorts of other stimuli, including all the sensory and informational input that we are chronically bombarded with daily.

The Gupta Program strengthens the function of the parasympathetic nervous system and helps promote relaxation and calm, thereby decreasing anxiety and bolstering the immune system. The support of the immune system decreases systemic inflammation in both the body and the brain and is very helpful when a patient is trying to wean off psychiatric medications.

The following are a few case examples of patients who came to see me who wished to discontinue medications. These patients were able to fully commit to implementing my recommendations and were able to successfully get off medications.

### *Craig reclaims his health and vitality*

Craig was a 44-year-old man who was the oldest of five children and the only boy born into a very patriarchal family system. His father was a wealthy authoritarian businessman who was volatile and violent, and his mother was passive and depressed. He had frequent sinus infections and bronchitis in childhood, was prescribed numerous courses of antibiotics, and once was hospitalized for asthma.

He was 12 years old when his parents divorced, and he became the man of the house. The responsibility of caring for his mother and sisters weighed heavily upon him, and he began to abuse substances as a young teenager. He became sober in his early 20s. His first hospitalization was at the age of 41 for a psychotic depression. By that time, he was married and had two children. The hospitalization was precipitated by his response to losing his job and the resulting overwhelming worries related to meeting the financial responsibilities for his family. This period also coincided with the death of a close friend.

During the hospitalization, he had a series of flashbacks of previously repressed memories from childhood. He recalled that, around the time of his parents' divorce, his father tried to kill his mother, and Craig had intervened. After he stabilized, he was discharged from the hospital on antipsychotic and antidepressant medications, which were eventually discontinued when he developed sexual side effects and gynecomastia (enlargement of the breast gland tissue in males). Sexual side effects frequently accompany the use of antidepressant medications and, contrary to what is commonly assumed, often persist well beyond the point when they are discontinued. Sexual dysfunction may take the form of decreased desire or difficulty with arousal and climax. When these medications are prescribed, this distressing side effect is unfortunately not often acknowledged or fully discussed.

Nine months after stopping the medications, he again became paranoid and suicidally depressed and was rehospitalized. He was discharged from the hospital on antipsychotic medication, which caused elevated blood sugar and cholesterol, weight gain, tiredness, muscle soreness, and exercise intolerance. Weight gain and metabolic syndrome are very common consequences of taking antipsychotic medications. He suffered from frequent headaches, brain fog, itching, anxiety, depression, and disrupted sleep. His psychiatrist was unwilling to work with him to wean from the medication because of his history of relapse with psychosis and suicidal ideation.

During our first meeting, he said that he had not enjoyed his career working in finance and had gone back to school to study family law and would soon be completing his degree. Due to his history of relapse, I asked that his wife accompany him to our next appointment so that, if she felt concerned as we lowered his dose of medication, she would know me and feel more comfortable reaching out. I wanted to ensure that she was supportive of the changes we were planning. Sometimes, family members are understandably quite fearful about reducing medications because of what they have been through in the past when their loved one relapsed.

Before I began the slow process of lowering the dosage of his antipsychotic, I asked him to follow the Wahls Protocol and to do the Gupta Program. He followed all my recommendations conscientiously, and after two months, we lowered his dose by 10 percent and continued to do so over the course of nine months. Sometimes, he would have trouble sleeping when we lowered the dose. At those times, he would take melatonin, and we would not further reduce the dose until he stabilized. Six months into our work together, while we were still in the process of slowly decreasing his medications, he reported that he felt like a completely different person from when we first met. He had lost the weight he gained on the medication; his muscles had stopped aching, which allowed him to exercise more; his sleep, energy, and mood had improved; and he no longer experienced headaches or brain fog. He began playing and enjoying music again and, by the time that he was completely off the medication, reported that he was feeling better than he had ever felt in his entire life.

Craig was a superstar. He conscientiously followed all my recommendations, which is not at all easy to do. It's quite challenging to follow a diet that does not include beloved foods, to exercise regularly, and to discipline yourself to do a 45-minute mind–body–spirit program daily. By the end of our time working together, he was very grateful that he felt so well. I had to remind him that he was the one who did all the work. I can have the best ideas in the world about what would be helpful, but if a patient does not follow my recommendations, it simply does not work. It needs to be a close cocreative partnership and, as you can see, takes a great deal of consistent effort to heal holistically.

## Aaron and lithium

Another patient who is still working with me to wean from antipsychotic medications is a 25-year-old man named Aaron. He is an extraordinarily creative, talented musician and composer who just graduated from college. I met monthly with Aaron and his parents as we very slowly tapered the high dose of antipsychotic medication that he was prescribed after he had been hospitalized twice for manic episodes. The first episode occurred when he suddenly stopped taking citalopram because he had lost his prescription refill. The sudden discontinuation of the antidepressant catapulted him into a florid manic state, and he was obliged to withdraw from the competitive music program in which he was enrolled. He has been mourning the loss of this opportunity ever since, and much of the emotional work has been to help him accept and grieve the ways his illness derailed his professional and personal development.

When he first came to see me, his appearance and demeanor were very constricted and flat, and he seemed quite sedated. My observation is that these medications often function like a chemical straitjacket that completely shuts down creativity and imagination. We began to work together with the aim of reducing his antipsychotic dose by 10 percent a month. Sometimes, it has been necessary to hold the dose steady because Aaron's mood needed more time to stabilize. Typically, 10 days after we reduce the dose, his mood dips, and he is more depressed for a week or so, and then he stabilizes, but not always. It has been important to be flexible and to respond to his clinical condition rather than to adhere to a rigid tapering schedule. His prescription must be compounded, because the medication is not available at a conventional pharmacy in incremental dosages. Aaron is another patient who follows all my recommendations. His parents are very dedicated and involved in helping him implement my suggestions. He adheres to an anti-inflammatory diet and exercises regularly.

He is also taking lithium carbonate as a mood stabilizer, and I am not recommending that he stop taking this. Over the years, I have had many patients who have had frank manic episodes, and I consider lithium carbonate to be protective against reoccurrence. It is an effective medication with a long history, and, in my experience, is underused in favor of newer, more expensive mood stabilizers. In areas of the world where there are trace amounts of naturally occurring lithium in the drinking water, there is a lower rate of suicide, as this seems to have a protective effect.[18]

## Lithium: a cost benefit analysis

Lithium is a natural mineral salt rather than a synthetic, manufactured compound like Prozac. Lithium carbonate is generally well tolerated, although some patients experience excessive thirst and urination or

---

18 Anjum Memon, Imogen Rogers, Sophie M. D. D. Fitzsimmons, Ben Carter, Rebecca Strawbridge, Diego Hidalgo-Mazzei, and Allan H. Young, "Association between Naturally Occurring Lithium in Drinking Water and Suicide Rates: Systematic Review and Meta-Analysis of Ecological Studies," *Journal of Psychiatry* 217 (2020): 667–678.

diarrhea at higher dosages, and for some, it can be harmful to the kidney and thyroid over time. Some patients report that they feel that their experience is "grayed out." They do not feel things as intensely and do not like this feeling.

Treatment with lithium carbonate is often accompanied by side effects and is not without risk. Unfortunately, I do not have other natural treatments to offer that compare in terms of efficacy. Other mood stabilizers have even more adverse side effects than lithium carbonate. The need for a mood stabilizer in patients who have had recurrent episodes of mania is not, in my mind, debatable. Frank mania is a psychiatric emergency that puts a patient at tremendous risk. Patients in a manic state often have very poor judgment, are disinhibited, and can behave in ways that cause them a great deal of shame and suffering when they recover. They can ruin their professional reputation, do significant damage to themselves financially, engage in risky sexual behavior, and deeply traumatize the people who love them. Although it is heartbreaking to prescribe medications to my patients that can make them feel diminished and cause side effects or that can even do harm to their organs, in the case of lithium carbonate, the benefit clearly outweighs the risk.

It is also true and important to acknowledge that bipolar disorder is overdiagnosed, and patients are frequently inappropriately placed permanently on mood stabilizers that have serious side effects. When a careful history is elicited, I often disagree with the diagnosis. The most frequent confusion seems to be with an acute post-traumatic reaction or a drug-induced psychotic state, and their symptoms do not represent mania in the context of classic bipolar disorder. This is important to differentiate and is particularly dangerous for children. It is not uncommon that an angry, traumatized child who is not sleeping is diagnosed as bipolar and prescribed mood stabilizers.

I have had patients ask whether they could take the over-the-counter nutraceutical lithium orotate instead, but in my experience, it is in no way an equivalent substitute. Many claims have been made about its efficacy, but that has not been born out in my practice. It can be somewhat helpful in terms of mood regulation but does not offer real protection against mania like lithium carbonate does. A dose of lithium orotate contains about 5–10 mg of lithium, whereas most of my patients are taking 600–1,200 mg of lithium carbonate.

A manic episode is almost always tremendously destructive and painful to the individual and their family and friends. One of the most damaging consequences of a manic episode is related to a patient's sense of themselves. Patients who have had manic episodes often lose trust in themselves and often live in fear that it will happen again, which is true for their loved ones as well. Family members and friends often develop a post-traumatic response to what would otherwise be an average and not alarming fluctuation in the mood of the person who has a history of mania. Most of us can have a bad day and feel quite depressed or anxious without worrying that it spells the beginning of a dangerous, spiraling loss of control and of behavior that will occasion enormous feelings of shame and regret when we return to a baseline state of mind. The same reaction can be had in response to natural feelings of joy or excitement in a person with a history of mania. The observation of unusually happy feelings can provoke fears about getting "high," as well as terror about what a poor night's sleep might portend. We may all feel unpleasantly tired if we do not sleep well, but we do not worry that it is the harbinger of a much more worrisome situation. I have witnessed Aaron's parents become very fearful when there is a dip in his mood or when he gets overfocused on an idea that is not reasonable. It triggers frightening, terrible memories of when he was psychotic and hospitalized and it took several years for him to return to his former self.

## Gemmotherapy

The conventional psychopharmacologic approaches for Aaron are augmented with a treatment modality called *gemmotherapy*. *Gemmo* is related to the Latin word *gammae*, which means "bud." Gemmotherapy is a natural treatment that makes use of the healing properties inherent in the embryonic tissue in growing plants, the buds and new shoots of trees and shrubs. It was invented by Pol Henry, a Belgium homeopath in the 1960s, who called it *phytembryotherapy*. It is a comprehensive energetic cell therapy that has remarkable therapeutic potential.

Buds are embryonic tissue that contains all the genetic heritage of the future plant. They are filled with vibrant, condensed essential energy and all the requisite ingredients required for the budding plant to mature. Gemmos are nontoxic and act upon a person's organism on multiple levels, including the body, mind, heart, and spirit. They bear similarity to homeopathy but are not identical. Gemmos are extracts of the macerated plant tissue mixed with alcohol and glycerin and are mixed into water in tiny doses, only one to five drops up to twice a day. Gemmos are used much more commonly in Europe than in this country. In Europe, the black currant gemmo is the most prescribed and can be helpful for inflammation. Aaron is currently taking field maple, which has properties that support the stabilization of his mood, and olive gemmo to ease the grip of recurring, distorted, negative thoughts about his body. He is currently thriving. He's excited about his creative work, interested in dating, and planning to teach music next year.

## Benzodiazepines

I have helped many patients wean off benzodiazepines, which can be very challenging. As I mentioned previously, these medications are highly addictive, and the taper must be done slowly and cautiously, or else the patient will usually suffer unbearable anxiety. Again, in these situations, an anti-inflammatory diet and mind–body practices to calm the nervous system are essential for success. I have met a number of patients who entered rehab facilities in order to wean from benzodiazepines, but this is not an endeavor that can be accomplished in a 21-day stay. It typically requires a year or more to do so safely without causing distress.

The titration schedule to wean off the medication needs to be very flexible, and there is no rushing the process. The dosage can be reduced by obtaining incrementally lower dosages from a compounding pharmacy or switching the patient from their current benzodiazepine to an equivalent amount of diazepam (Valium), which comes in a 2 mg tablet. Heather Ashton wrote an invaluable monograph on how benzodiazepines work and how to taper safely from them. Her work contains multiple conversion tables for various benzodiazepines and the equivalent dosage of diazepam. Her monograph is called *The Ashton Manual*.

## Spiritual considerations

Although it may seem like this discussion of weaning from medications is all about the physical body and mundane considerations, all our experiences have the potential to provide us with opportunities for spiritual growth and development. As I have described, the process of discontinuing prescription medications can be extremely challenging. As such, it is perfectly designed for deepening the spiritual practice of connecting more regularly with ancestors and guides and asking for assistance, performing rituals and ceremonies, and making use of all the tools we've discussed so far.

I recommend to all my patients who are open to these practices to make regular offerings in the spirit of giving thanks, to focus on gratitude and blessings rather than on what is lacking, and to constantly ask for guidance and support as they navigate this challenging journey. It can also be helpful to find regular opportunities to be of service to others, which is uplifting and allows the patient to turn the focus momentarily away from personal distress and sorrows.

I hope that this brief discussion of the application of spiritual principles to a topic that, on the surface, is just about the physical body will open your mind to the ways in which you can avail yourself of spiritual assistance when going through trying and difficult experiences.

*Chapter Seven*

# MAST CELL ACTIVATION SYNDROME, MOLD TOXICITY, AND EHLERS–DANLOS SYNDROMES

> As any doctor can tell you, the most crucial step toward healing is having the right diagnosis. If the disease is precisely identified, a good resolution is far more likely. Conversely, a bad diagnosis usually means a bad outcome, no matter how skilled the physician.
>
> —ANDREW WEIL, MD

In addition to the usual symptoms of depression, anxiety, insomnia, and attentional problems that frequently inspire a consultation with a psychiatrist, many patients who seek my help are also suffering from chronic mysterious illnesses characterized by diverse and fluctuating symptoms that afflict multiple organ systems. Chronic debilitating fatigue is common, as is chronic pain in many parts of the body, including the bones, tendons, and muscles. Heart and respiratory issues, such as palpitations and arrhythmias, as well as asthma and frequent sinus infections, are common. Patients often report digestive symptoms, such as diarrhea, constipation, bloating, and reflux, and peculiar neurological symptoms such as numbness and tingling in various parts of their body; visual symptoms; hypersensitivity to light, touch, sound, smells, foods, chemicals, and electromagnetic frequencies (EMF); difficulties with dizziness and balance; ringing in the ears; and headaches. Cognitive symptoms such as brain fog, difficulty concentrating, and memory problems are also common. Many patients report rashes and hives, itchiness, and swollen lymph nodes, as well as severe symptoms accompanying menstruation, including very heavy periods, painful cramps, and premenstrual syndrome. Some report pelvic pain and interstitial cystitis, a painful, inflammatory condition of the bladder.

## It's not all in their head

When a patient who seeks help from a doctor and reports symptoms that refer to multiple unrelated organ systems that do not fit with known patterns or conditions and when the tests that are conventionally run do not reveal any abnormality, the conclusion that is usually reached is that this patient should see a psychiatrist. They are told that they are suffering from stress; that they are depressed or anxious; that their condition is psychosomatic, meaning that their emotions are manifesting as physical symptoms; and that there is nothing measurably abnormal in terms of the laboratory studies. The patients, on the other hand, are certain that there is something terribly wrong, but their doctor cannot figure it out and they are told that it is all in their head.

This is a very invalidating experience, which adds insult to injury. These patients are often depressed and anxious because the inflammation that is affecting their entire body is also affecting their brain and because of the desperation in response to living with disabling symptoms for which they cannot get any help. If they do see a psychiatrist, they will be offered an antidepressant or antianxiety medication or a stimulant to treat their attentional problems and brain fog and not much else. That is the standard of care, meaning that is how similarly qualified practitioners would manage the patient's care under the same or similar circumstances.

When a patient calls me and reports multiple symptoms like the ones previously listed, my first thought diagnostically is that they are suffering from mast cell activation syndrome (MCAS), and the most common underlying cause is mold toxicity.

## Mast cell activation syndrome

Mast cells are white blood cells that are part of the immune system and that function as a bridge between the immune and the nervous system, acting to coordinate between the two. Their primary function is to defend against toxins and infectious agents. Mast cells can be found in all tissues of the body, but the highest concentrations are in those parts of the body that interface with the outside world and are thus exposed to infections and toxins. These include the sinuses, throat, gastrointestinal tract, respiratory tract, skin, and genitourinary tract.

Mast cells are filled with vesicles called *granules* that contain more than 200 different biochemical signalers, such as histamine, serotonin, tryptase, cytokines, interleukins, prostaglandins, and chemokines. When a toxin or infectious agent is introduced, an individual with a well-functioning immune system will mobilize their mast cells to orchestrate an appropriately measured response. The mast cells release their biochemical mediators to neutralize the danger. This is an important natural defense function of the immune system. If a person's immune system has become dysregulated and hyperaroused, the mast cells can become overreactive. Instead of releasing their biochemical mediators in an appropriately self-limited way, they become disorganized and degranulate chaotically, causing the wide array of symptoms listed earlier.

Treatment consists of stabilizing the membranes of the mast cells so that they do not degranulate, and calming down the nervous system. For some patients, conventional over-the-counter antihistamines, H1 blockers, can be useful, such as Claritin, Allegra, or Zyrtec. For seasonal allergies, it is recommended that these antihistamines be taken once a day. To treat MCAS, they are taken twice a day. Sometimes, the antihistamine needs to be compounded, because the fillers in these over-the-counter antihistamines can cause adverse reactions. A person may not be able to tolerate Claritin because it makes them sleepy, but Allegra does not. It is a matter of trial and error to determine which antihistamine will be most helpful. They are not helpful for everyone and can make some people feel worse. Improvement may be immediate or can take up to two months. Pepcid, an H2 blocker, starting with 20 mg before bedtime and increasing the dosage to twice daily if tolerated, is added after starting the Allegra, Zyrtec, or Claritin.

## *Mast cell stabilization*

Natural treatments for mast cell stabilization include 500 mg of Quercetin, a flavonoid that is a member of the vitamin C family. It is typically taken three times a day: 30 minutes before meals and before bedtime. Some patients do not tolerate it either. Other supplements that can be useful are Neuroprotek, which is a combination of three flavonoids (quercetin, luteolin, and rutin), and Mirica, which is a combination of luteolin and palmitoylethanolamine, which is a lipid that has an anti-inflammatory effect. There are other natural substances that can be helpful, such as Perimine, an extract of the perilla seed;

histamine digestive enzymes, such as HistDAO, which contains the enzyme diamine oxidase and which is taken 30 minutes before each meal to help break down histamine; and AllQlear, a tryptase blocker, which is derived from quail eggs. It is also taken 30 minutes before each meal. Prescription medications for MCAS include ketotifen and cromolyn sodium.

Most patients with MCAS also have limbic system dysregulation, a malfunction of the deep structures of the brain that is a trauma response and that results in an individual feeling in a constant state of hyperarousal, of fight, flight, or freeze. The Gupta Program is a highly researched mind–body–spirit practice that is extremely helpful and effective in calming down the limbic system.

I regularly recommend that my patients with MCAS commit to doing the Gupta Program daily. This is an essential component of healing. A negative feedback loop exists between the limbic system and the mast cells, and when the limbic system is dysregulated, it causes the mast cells to degranulate, creating the symptoms associated with MCAS. Similarly, the mast cells degranulating further dysregulates the limbic system. Those patients with multiple chemical sensitivities or those who are extraordinarily sensitive to light or sound or hypersensitive to EMFs, or those who have adverse reactions to many different foods—at times including even a glass of water—are all suffering from MCAS and can benefit from treatments to stabilize the mast cells, particularly limbic system retraining programs like the Gupta Program.

For some patients, the thought of committing to a daily 45-minute mind–body–spirit practice is daunting and overwhelming. They are willing to take supplements, but it feels too onerous to have to make the time daily to do guided meditations and practices. These patients are less likely to heal from MCAS quickly. I recommend that if 45 minutes is too much, then they can start with 10 minutes and work their way up. It's important that they determine how to make it work for them and to include it in their daily healing plan. There is another limbic retraining program that is equivalent to the Gupta Program called the Dynamic Neural Retraining System. Which system a patient prefers is a matter of taste; they both do the same thing and are both effective. These days, most of my patients seem to prefer the Gupta Program, which is more flexible and less demanding. Energy healing sessions with modalities such as BodyIntuitive can also be of benefit.

## *Some may benefit from a low-histamine diet*

Some patients with MCAS benefit from a low-histamine diet. It is important to determine whether this does, in fact, make a difference, because it is not pleasurable or healthful to restrict the diet unnecessarily. If a low-histamine diet does not result in improvement, it should not be continued. A low-histamine diet is not like a gluten-free diet, because it is not possible to totally avoid histamine in our food. It is analogous to the situation where a person who has an addiction to food cannot avoid eating, in contrast to an alcoholic who can completely abstain from alcohol. Most foods contain histamine. In sensitive individuals, when the level of histamine reaches a certain threshold, symptoms then develop. Imagine a bucket is filled with histamine when you consume foods. When the bucket is full, it overflows, and symptoms develop.

The Histamine Intolerance Awareness (HIA) website provides a list of problematic foods.[19] There are many such lists available on the internet, and they are not all in agreement with one another. When it comes down to it, it's a matter of trial and error. This can be

---

19 www.histamineintolerance.org.uk/about/the-food-diary/the-food-list

particularly frustrating, because food intolerances can fluctuate. At one point, avocados can be safely consumed, and then a month later, you may find that you are having an adverse reaction. Some foods contain high levels of histamine, others are histamine liberators that cause histamine contained in our own cells to be released, and some block the enzyme that breaks down histamine, resulting in elevated levels. Here is the HIA list:

**High-histamine foods**

- Alcohol
- Pickled or canned foods, sauerkrauts
- Matured cheeses
- Smoked meat products: salami, ham, sausages, and so forth.
- Shellfish
- Beans and pulses: chickpeas, soybeans, peanuts
- Nuts: walnuts, cashews
- Chocolates and other cocoa-based products
- Most citric fruits
- Wheat-based products
- Vinegar
- Prepared meals
- Salty snacks, sweets with preservatives and artificial colorings

**Histamine liberators**

- Most citric fruits: kiwi, lemon, lime, pineapple, plums
- Cocoa and chocolate

- Nuts
- Papaya
- Beans and pulses
- Tomatoes
- Wheat germ
- Additives: benzoate, sulphites, nitrites, glutamate, food dyes

**Diamine oxidase blockers**

- Alcohol
- Black tea
- Energy drinks
- Green tea
- Mate tea

**Debatable**

- Yogurt: depends on the bacteria culture used
- Egg white: a histamine liberator only when in its raw state

**Other**

- Yeast: even though it does not contain histamine as such, yeast serves as a catalyst for histamine generation during manufacture

Leftovers can also develop high levels of histamine, and eating only freshly cooked food makes a difference for some people. One strategy is to make a large portion of food and then freeze smaller portions in glass containers. This is called *batch cooking*.

I mentioned a class of digestive enzymes previously, the diamine oxidase supplements, which break down histamine. It can be helpful for some individuals to take this type of supplement 15 minutes before a meal to lower the level of histamine in the bucket.

MCAS can have so many different causes. It may be the result of chronic Lyme disease or other tick-borne illnesses like bartonella. It can be a manifestation of a post-COVID syndrome and is likely responsible for many of the symptoms of long COVID. It can be activated by other viral conditions, such as Epstein-Barr virus or can occur as a consequence of emotional or physical trauma, a car accident, or a head injury. In my practice, by far the most common cause of MCAS is mold toxicity.

## The dangers of electromagnetic radiation

All of us are sensitive to electromagnetic radiation, and it has a deleterious effect upon our health, but some patients with MCAS are particularly sensitive, and limiting their exposure can make a huge difference in the severity of their symptoms.

Prior to 200 years ago, our only exposure to electromagnetic radiation came from sunlight and other cosmic sources, lightning, and geomagnetic forces. That is not the case today. Electricity and our capacity to store it are the foundation of modern civilization. Electricity has enabled all the staggering rapid technological and scientific advancement of the modern era. The applications of electromagnetic technology, however, has resulted in our ever-increasing bombardment and exposure to higher frequencies and dosages of radiation. Humans cannot see, touch, taste, or smell this radiation, which understandably contributes to our capacity to deny the risks of exposure. Its effects accrue over time and are proportional to the duration and intensity of exposure.

Some EMFs cause damage to our intricate and delicate DNA and are related to the development of cancers, cardiovascular disease, diabetes, neurodegenerative diseases, infertility, depression, and suicide. "Scientists, doctors, and researchers have long accepted that ionizing radiation, such as the ultraviolet rays that accompany sunlight or the X-rays that you are exposed to in your doctor's or dentist's office, can harm and destroy DNA. It has been assumed, however, that nonionizing radiation from power lines, television broadcasting, and cell phones did not harm DNA."[20] This is not the case. Nonionizing radiation can react with and harm DNA, which can cause mutations and even cell death and can lead directly to serious medical illness.

Just as the tobacco industry suppressed the scientific evidence regarding the hazards of cigarette smoking, there is a profit-motivated strategy to manufacture doubt about the negative health effects of wireless technology. There has been a repeated assertion that there is no "proven link" between wireless frequencies and human illness, that the data is inconclusive. "It appears that the response of governments and industry groups to this lack of specific cause and effect relationship between nonthermal exposure to EMF and negative health effects has been to formulate regulations and safety standards that ignore those negative effects completely. While there is plenty of science indicating the presence of significant health risks at nonthermal levels, as far as safety standards and regulatory frameworks are concerned, EMF is harmful to humans only at levels powerful enough to result in increased temperature (the so-called thermal effect). No recognition at all is given to any potential health effects at lower, nonthermal levels of nonionizing

---

20 Martin Blank, *Overpowered: What Science Tells Us about the Dangers of Cell Phones and Other Wi-Fi Devices* (Seven Stories Press, 2015), p. 51.

electromagnetic radiation even though nonthermal biological effects have been scientifically demonstrated for over a century."[21]

There are two key principles: First, minimize your use of EMF-generating technology. Next, maximize the distance between you and those EMF sources when they are in use.

Here is a partial list of some of the steps that you can take to reduce your exposure. I know that these recommendations can feel like an unwelcome hassle. But it's important. Making even small changes can make a difference cumulatively. I always talk with my patients about EMF hygiene to minimize their exposure.

- Do not live near high-voltage power lines
- Stay away from transformers
- Live as far from cell phone antennas as possible
- Don't use electric blankets or waterbeds
- Run extension cords away from furniture, and keep the cords organized
- Switch from electric to battery alarm clocks
- Energy-efficient appliances generate less pollution than older, less-efficient models
- Don't use fluorescent lights
- Don't use dimmers of three-way switches
- Don't use microwaves, but if you do, get out of the kitchen when the microwave is on
- Put your cell phone on airplane mode when it is not in use
- Don't put your cell phone in your pocket

---

21 Blank, *Overpowered*, 161.

- Laptops are not for laps
- Minimize the use of hairdryers and electric razors
- Consider using an ethernet cable rather than Wi-Fi in your home
- Turn the Wi-Fi router off at night
- Switch to plastic eyeglass frames and foam mattresses that do not function as antennas

## Mold toxicity

Prior to 2016, illness related to mold exposure was something that I had heard of but did not know much about. I did not recognize the powerful disabling impact it can have upon the immune system. In the fall of 2016, I started a Kundalini yoga teacher training, which required a daily home practice. I set up my yoga props in a cozy corner of the carpeted finished basement and practiced there for at least an hour every day. Kundalini yoga often involves long, deep breathing, as well as a rapid breath pattern called *the breath of fire*. After about two weeks of inhaling the basement air, I began to feel an overwhelmingly heightened sense of anxiety and profound depression and began to wake up multiple times throughout the night. I also experienced bloating, headaches, and tinnitus. I was baffled, because I could identify no obvious precipitant.

A few weeks prior to the onset of my symptoms, one of the readers of my blog wrote to me and mentioned that she had been diagnosed with toxic mold and thought that I might be interested in the topic. She wrote, "I am going to bet that many of your psych patients have this mold-based illness and that you will love this info and find it very useful in your practice." I wrote her back, thanked her, and said that I looked forward to learning more about it.

I stopped going down to the basement to do yoga. I don't know why; I must have been feeling too miserable to practice. But a few days later, my anxiety started to melt away, the depression lifted, and I started sleeping through the night. After three days, I felt completely fine again. Suddenly, I remembered the email, reread it, and began to wonder whether toxic mold had been causing me to feel so awful. The growth of toxic mold is initiated by water damage, and there had been flooding in my basement several years previously. Testing the basement revealed very high levels of mold, and I was obliged to go through a very expensive process of professional remediation.

Mold toxicity is not recognized as a legitimate diagnosis by conventional medicine. Part of the reason is that vulnerability to mold toxicity is only present in perhaps 25 percent of the population, who, for a variety of reasons, do not have a robust detoxification system. One of the primary biochemical processes involved in detoxification is methylation, and the people who are susceptible to developing mold toxicity do not methylate well. A family can be living in a water-damaged house together, but only one family member will become ill. This is because that person is the only one who cannot effectively metabolize and detoxify the mold toxins. The conventional perspective of mold deniers is that if mold were really a problem, then everyone in the house would get sick, and thus the problem is discounted. Conventional medicine, for the most part, does not recognize mold toxicity as a cause of chronic illness and does not believe that the urinalysis that tests for mycotoxins is reliable or meaningful or that the treatments are valid or indicated. Colleagues with knowledge of environmentally acquired illness have a completely different impression and find that treating mold toxicity has a profound impact on the health of the immune system and well-being.

Mold allergies and mold toxicity are not the same illness. Mold allergies are due to mold spores that are inhaled and that cause hay-fever-like symptoms. It is different from toxic mold, which is due to the volatile toxic vapors produced by mold that can cause MCAS due to poor clearance of bio toxins. It can manifest with so many different and diverse symptoms that it is frequently misdiagnosed. It is likely that many cases of chronic fatigue, fibromyalgia, MCAS and histamine intolerance, irritable bowel and leaky gut, multiple sclerosis, and chronic Lyme that does not respond to treatment are due to toxic mold causing a chronic inflammatory response. Unfortunately, most conventional practitioners and even alternative practitioners do not include it as a possibility. It should absolutely be on the list of possible treatable causes of medical and psychiatric symptoms.

Toxic mold is a more prevalent and a more serious problem than ever before. Due to common building practices of using drywall or sheetrock, which was not a material that was used in construction in the past, more people are now being exposed to toxic mold. Drywall is a great medium for mold growth. The current practice of making homes more energy efficient means that there is less ventilation from outside air, and the toxic mold gasses can be trapped inside, potentiating their effect. There is also research that EMFs cause mold to release its toxins in self-defense. The Wi-Fi routers that are so common in our homes may also cause mold to become more virulent. In addition, in the 1970s, antifungals were added to paint, which stimulated the mold to mutate and become more dangerous. Of course, the impact of climate change and the greatly increased incidence of flooding is a setup for the development of severe mold issues.

Treatment of mold toxicity starts with drawing the mold toxins out of the body with a variety of binders, such as charcoal, clay, chlorella, and cholestyramine, an old cholesterol-lowering medication. Without pretreating with binders, a patient would likely feel very sick as the fungus dies off when exposed to antifungal medications. It is important to proceed slowly. After a patient has been on binders for six to eight weeks, treatment with antifungals is initiated. Antifungals can be used to target the mold colonization in the gut or the respiratory system or both, depending on a patient's symptoms. Other supplements are also recommended, such as biofilm dissolvers and colloidal silver, as well as TUDCA (tauroursodeoxycholic acid), a supplement that enhances the flow of bile and helps the body excrete the biotoxins. Most important is that the treatment be undertaken slowly and cautiously. Patients who are in a big hurry to get the treatment over with and thus heroically take large doses of binders rather than increasing incrementally often regret it and can actually make themselves sicker.

## The miracle of synchronicity

The more I learned about toxic mold, the more grateful I was that avoiding the moldy basement was all I needed to do to recover. This is not the case for many people. Mold toxins can accumulate in the body, continuing to wreak havoc long after exposure ceases and requiring an extensive and often arduous course of treatment. But, for everyone, the first and most crucial step in treatment is to identify the source of the mold and to get away from it. So many buildings in this country are water damaged, including schools, and kids are being exposed to biotoxins in the environment that degrade cognition, attention, and memory. I believe that many patients coming to psychiatrists with anxiety, depression, cognitive and attentional problems, insomnia, and brain fog are actually suffering from the consequences of exposure to toxic mold.

My awakening to the enormous problem of toxic mold is an example of synchronicity, evidence of a nonrandom meaningful Universe. Had I not begun Kundalini yoga teacher training, I would not have been breathing deeply in the basement daily for an hour and fallen ill. Had that generous reader not written to me at that moment to share her discovery, I would not have connected the dots about toxic mold causing my debilitating psychiatric and physical symptoms. Had I not connected the dots, my consciousness would not have been raised about this common and very important underlying cause of psychiatric symptoms, and I would not have known what was afflicting my patients and how to help. The Universe provides all of us with endless opportunities to help one another if we are open to allowing the mystery to work through us.

## Ehlers–Danlos syndromes

The Ehlers–Danlos syndromes (EDS) are a collection of genetic disorders that weaken and undermine the normal structure and function of collagen, a protein produced by the body that is an essential component of skin, cartilage, bones, tendons, ligaments, blood and lymphatic vessels, and connective tissues. Since these tissues are found all over the body, every organ system can be affected, and, therefore, the presentation and symptoms of this illness can be extremely varied.

Pain and fatigue, however, are experienced almost universally by patients with EDS. Many of these patients also have MCAS and mold toxicity and thus suffer from the wide array of psychiatric symptoms, such as depression, anxiety, phobias, insomnia, attentional issues, and brain fog, that are associated with these diagnoses. It is therefore very common for EDS patients to seek help from a psychiatrist. Unfortunately, most psychiatrists do not recognize this disorder. This is not only true for psychiatrists but for other medical professionals as well. Physicians may have a vague memory of learning about EDS years ago in medical school but remember only that it is a genetic disorder with hypermobility.

EDS is so very common in my practice that, in the intake paperwork that I send to patients prior to our initial meeting, I also include a checklist of symptoms related to connective tissue abnormalities. It can be an enormous relief when I raise the possibility of this diagnosis as an explanation for the collection of strange and mysterious symptoms that have plagued them for as long as they can remember. Their symptoms are potentially related to a single cause—namely, an abnormality of the connective tissue. These patients often have histories of extensive contact with the medical system over the course of their lifetimes, because they have a history of chronic illness. Sometimes they have been told that they have chronic fatigue or fibromyalgia, both of which are vague, wastebasket diagnoses that really are only descriptive, meaning that the patients are exhausted (chronic fatigue) or that they have pain all over their body (fibromyalgia).

## *A spectrum disorder*

Some disorders, such as autism, are spectrum disorders. This means that there are some children who are severely afflicted, who are nonverbal and prone to engagement in repetitive self-stimulating behaviors, and that there are others who are only mildly afflicted. These children may simply demonstrate a lack of interest or capacity in interpersonal relationships or may have an encyclopedic knowledge of and obsessive fascination with a particular subject—for example, trains or the weather.

Clinically, EDS is also a spectrum disorder. Many of the patients I see do not have the full-blown dramatic syndrome with identifiable genetics, but they are still suffering from many of the symptoms that are related to an abnormality of their collagen and connective tissue. They may have extreme hypermobility in some of their joints, such as the capacity to bend their thumb backward and touch their wrist or to touch their hands flat to the floor with their knees straight or hyperextend their elbows. Some may bruise easily or suffer from chronic constipation, dizziness, and elevated heart rate when they rise from sitting to standing (postural orthostatic hypotension or POTS), but they are not necessarily constantly dislocating joints and injuring themselves like someone with a severe version of EDS. They also do not have a history of prolapsed or ruptured organs and vessels, nor do they have eye or dental problems. This milder type is technically called *hypermobile spectrum disorder*, rather than hypermobile EDS.

There are 13 different inherited subtypes of EDS that have been identified. The two known genetic modes of inheritance are autosomal dominant and autosomal recessive. All the types can have joint hypermobility (joints that move farther than normal), subluxations (partial dislocation) and deformity of joints, frequent injuries, scoliosis, skin hyperelasticity (skin that stretches more than normal), velvety skin, poor wound healing, abnormal scarring, and tissue weakness that can lead to hernias and prolapses of organs, eye disease, gum and dental disease, cardiovascular disease, and life-threatening ruptures of vessels and organs. Often, there are digestive symptoms, such as constipation due to abnormal peristalsis (involuntary wavelike movements of contraction and relaxation of the musculature of the intestinal tract that propel the food forward), nausea, vomiting, difficulty swallowing, reflux, bloating, and food intolerances. Autonomic instability is a common feature characterized by disturbances in heart rate, blood pressure, and temperature regulation.

## *The tragic consequence of misdiagnosis*

When a patient who is suffering from EDS sees an internist, pediatrician, or family practice doctor, the doctor is likely to run many tests and do many laboratory studies, none of which show anything treatable. There is indeed an underlying organic cause of the constellation of mysterious symptoms—that is, the abnormal structure and function of collagen—but, since this is not recognized, it cannot be addressed.

When the patient's distressing symptoms are not alleviated, and they are not getting any answers or effective treatment, they may become more insistent about something being very wrong, which can lead to a serious conflict between the patient and the clinician. Eventually, the frustrated clinician will often refer them to a psychiatrist or other mental health professional for counseling. They may be given a diagnosis of conversion disorder, defined as a psychological condition in which a person has blindness, paralysis, or other neurological symptoms that cannot be explained by medical evaluation. The traditional psychoanalytic understanding of conversion disorder is that it is a physical manifestation of unresolved conflict due to unbearable or unacceptable thoughts or feelings. This is obviously very invalidating and psychologically damaging for the patient and denies the fact that their symptoms are a direct result of an organic problem.

It is even more tragic when the patient is a child, and the parent desperately tries to find an answer or solution to their child's many medical symptoms by seeking consultation with one doctor after another. This parent eventually runs the risk of being diagnosed with factitious disorder, formerly called *Munchausen syndrome by proxy*. This diagnosis is understood as a form of child abuse, where the needy, attention-seeking caretaker (usually the mother) either makes up fictitious symptoms or literally causes real symptoms to make it look like the child is sick. Her motivation is thought to be the secondary gain, the perceived external advantages or benefits that may be derived as a result of having symptoms. This is akin to other historically outrageous formulations, such as the former psychoanalytic misunderstanding of autism as being due to having a "refrigerator mother." The autistic child's abnormal development was understood to result from maternal coldness and lack of caring, rather than a poorly understood organic brain disorder. This condition is due at least in part to a lack of capacity to detoxify an overload of toxins and has absolutely nothing to do with the quality of parent–child relating.

Not only is this type of misdiagnosis a sin of commission, in that it directly causes psychological damage, but it also results in sins of omission. The symptoms of EDS can be treated supportively with physical interventions if they are properly diagnosed.

## *Autonomic dysfunction*

Dysautonomia, in particular, is often misdiagnosed as a psychiatric disorder because it can present symptomatically as anxiety, panic, attention deficit disorder, and hypomania. Autonomic dysfunction results from a depletion of energy reserves due to chronic sympathetic nervous system overdrive. These patients often have very poor sleep quality due to chronic pain, which then leads to daytime fatigue, exhaustion, and poor stress resilience. This depletion puts them into survival mode and further activates their sympathetic nervous system, resulting in a state of chronic fight or flight.

Chronic hyperarousal can create the appearance of a generalized anxiety disorder, or if the patient has surges of adrenaline due to autonomic dysfunction, they can appear to be having a panic attack. This state of sympathetic hyperarousal can manifest as restlessness or hyperactivity, which can be mistaken for attention deficit hyperactivity disorder. Sometimes, the patient's ability to power through and to continue to function on very little sleep is mistaken for hypomania. Since they are so tired, they often make mistakes, misplace things, and have trouble concentrating and thus look like they are suffering from attention deficit disorder.

Psychiatric diagnoses are generally diagnoses of exclusion, meaning that the condition does not qualify if it is a consequence of an underlying medical problem. If a patient is sleeping poorly due to chronic pain as a result of EDS, they are exhausted, and their cognition is consequently impaired, it is inappropriate to diagnose attention deficit disorder. If they did have a good night's sleep, they would not be forgetful or have trouble concentrating. When they are referred to a psychiatrist, due to the ignorance of the actual underlying medical cause of their condition, they are routinely prescribed psychiatric medication. This can sometimes be helpful, but more often, it will either do nothing or make their symptoms worse. In addition, dysautonomia does respond to appropriate treatment, which consists of efforts to improve sleep quality, control chronic pain, provide adequate salt and fluid intake, avoid hypoglycemia, effectively manage stress, and get adequate rest. Without identifying the underlying cause, appropriate treatment will not be offered.

If EDS is suspected, genetic testing can be done. There is no cure for EDS, but the symptoms can be addressed and appropriately supported. It can be very helpful and relieving for patients to have a framework for understanding their condition. Unfortunately, due to the EDS illiteracy of most medical professionals, a patient suffering from EDS often goes undiagnosed, and, therefore, appropriate treatment is not offered.

## Immune system modulators

There is one pharmaceutical that I routinely recommend to patients who are suffering from any type of autoimmune illness, MCAS, or EDS: low-dose naltrexone. It is safe, inexpensive, and, for some patients, makes a huge difference in pain reduction and systemic inflammation. In my mind, this makes it always worth a trial.

Many people have heard of naltrexone, which is a medication used to reduce cravings for opioids and alcohol by blocking the opioid receptors. It can be obtained from a conventional pharmacy and is typically prescribed in doses of 50 mg three times a day. Unfortunately, it is generally poorly tolerated by patients because it blocks not only the effects of the intoxicants but also the effects of naturally occurring endorphins in the body, which leads to low mood and feelings of malaise. Most patients do not like how it makes them feel and eventually refuse to take it. Endorphins are naturally occurring neurotransmitters that create a feeling of well-being, such as the euphoria experienced by long-distance runners. Endorphins also play an important role in modulating the immune response and in reducing pain and inflammation.

Low-dose naltrexone is prescribed at doses between 0.25 to 4.5 mg daily, rather than 150 mg a day. At these low doses, the medication briefly blocks the opioid receptors for a few hours. Subsequently, a rebound effect occurs, with increased production of endorphins, resulting in an enhanced feeling of well-being, as well as a reduction in pain and systemic inflammation. Low-dose naltrexone appears to stabilize the mast cells and to have immune-modulating effects.

There are usually very few side effects. The most common one is vivid dreams, which typically resolves after a few days but can recur when the dose is increased. Other side effects that have been reported include headaches, gastrointestinal symptoms, and insomnia. But these side effects are typically mild and transient, if in fact any are experienced at all.

Low-dose naltrexone appears to have immune-modulating effects. In some patients, it helps to stabilize the mast cells and decreases systemic inflammation. There are studies reporting its efficacy not only in classic autoimmune illnesses such as ulcerative colitis, rheumatoid arthritis, multiple sclerosis, and psoriasis, but also in diverse conditions such as cancer, fibromyalgia, chronic fatigue, histamine intolerance and MCAS, autism, chronic pain and complex regional pain syndrome, AIDS, PTSD, anxiety, and depression.

It cannot be obtained from a conventional pharmacy and must be compounded. I typically start at a dose of 0.5 and increase slowly up to 4.5 mg, as tolerated. The effective and tolerated dosage varies. Sometimes, a patient does well on 0.25 mg and no more than that, and other patients have a good result with 4.5 mg. The approach is individualized and a matter of trial and error.

## Spiritual considerations

When a person is feeling ill, when they are deeply fatigued, when their cognition is clouded by brain fog, or when they are experiencing chronic pain, they can have difficulty feeling open to connecting with their spirit. Ironically, during these times, spiritual guidance and support are needed more than ever. It has been my experience that most patients seem to need a certain minimum level of well-being to feel open to experiencing gratitude, to be in a state of appreciation for all the blessings, and to have the energy and bandwidth to consider offering themselves in service to others. Treating MCAS, mold toxicity, and EDS can support a person's physical being and provide the symptom relief that can open them to being available for spiritual connection.

A feedback loop is created by connecting spiritually, which uplifts, calms, and fortifies, which, in turn, facilitates further physical healing and well-being. At these times of transition and turmoil on the planet, physical well-being is foundational for cultivating the resilience and courage to meet these challenges and not to succumb to overwhelm and despair.

It is my hope that if you are suffering from a chronic mysterious illness, this discussion of some of the very common treatable causes will eventually result in proper diagnosis of what is going on and finding a practitioner who can help you. Without an accurate diagnosis, it's not possible to avail oneself of appropriate treatment. Unfortunately, if you approach your regular primary care physician and ask to be tested for toxic mold or suggest that your symptoms are due to MCAS, it is unlikely that your doctor will be knowledgeable or open. See the "Resources" section at the end of the book for other options.

*Chapter Eight*

# LIONS, CHIRON, AND HEALING

According to Rabbi Isaac Luria, sparks of holiness are lodged in all things. In order for creation to occur, shards of the divine fell into the world of matter, and it's the task of each person to redeem and to liberate the sacred that lies within everything. For stones, plants, animals, ourselves, a heavenly exile exists until the light returns unbroken to its source. The early Hasidic masters emphasized that each person has a unique mission to play in this cosmic process.[22]

## Choice, evolution, and divine timing

When I was 49 years old, in 2005, at the time of my Chiron return, I began to experience a marked, accelerated period of spiritual growth and development, catalyzed by the end of my marriage and the death of both of my parents all within three months of each other. The grief

---

22  Edward Hoffman, *The Kabbalah Deck* (Chronicle Books, 2000).

and anxiety that I felt at that time fueled my search for a way to make sense of and contain my experience of loss, which led me first to astrology and then other spiritual practices, as well as a more holistic approach to healing beyond the exclusively psychological. Maturation is often the fruit of adverse experiences and suffering because adaptation occasions new awareness and insight. Big transitions require courage, patience, endurance, and a need to tolerate uncertainty, because habitual, familiar structures no longer hold, and new ways of navigating the world must be created.

I regret that it took me almost 50 years to feel brave enough to embody a more genuine version of myself. I devoted decades to my training in psychiatry and psychoanalysis, out of loyalty to my father and my acute awareness about how deeply important my conventional success and status were to him. I was always so aware of my parents' suffering and wanted to make it better for them. I wish that I had begun to study holistic and energetic approaches, Chinese medicine and Ayurveda, herbalism and homeopathy, astrology, and shamanism when I was in my 20s. It was, however, not yet the season for me to embrace a more authentic Aquarian version of myself as a healer. The Chiron return provided the cosmic tail winds of support for me to address the core wound I carried related to unconscious survivor guilt and its attendant feelings of obligation to fulfill the expectations and wishes of loved ones. I also had to bear my fears of being judged not only as not enough but also as crazy. The archetypal symbolism of the lion in the Strength card and in the story of Androcles embodies soul qualities that support the growth and development of courage, greater authenticity, presence, and self-expression during these times of radical change.

## The Strength card

In the Rider–Waite tarot deck, number eight is the Strength card. It pictures a graceful woman in a white dress with a wreath of flowers encircling her head and a lemniscate, or infinity symbol, hovering above her. Her hands are tenderly and compassionately encircling the face of an orange lion, and the background of the card is a bright, sunny yellow. The lemniscate symbolizes the flow between the conscious and unconscious, between heaven and earth, between our animal and spiritual natures. One flows into and interpenetrates the other, and they are in constant relationship.

The symbolism of the Strength card evokes the mythology of the figure of the centaur Chiron, who is half human and half horse. Chiron's form reminds us that we are both multidimensional and embodied beings. The modern mindset denigrates all matter, including the body, which is seen as inert, without spirit or innate intelligence. The Strength card reminds us of the intimate connection between Heaven and Earth, that matter is imbued with spirit, and that we are infinite spiritual beings having a temporally finite embodied experience.

The Strength card portrays a human and an animal in a loving relationship. The quality of connection represented between the woman and the lion is one of love and respect and models a right relationship with the animals and other beings we share our planet with. This image also reminds us of our own animal nature, that our physical body needs regular attention and care, and to be holistically supported and attended to in the ways previously discussed.

Without appropriate care of the physical body, we are much less able to feel expansive and spacious and to connect with what is greater than our small selves. Our bodies hold the memory of our personal history, everything we have experienced, including all the trauma we have endured, which is unconsciously stored and encoded in our tissues. This card represents that relationship between the conscious and unconscious.

Navigating these times skillfully requires that we tune into our bodies and hear its messages to us and receive the communication from this unconscious aspect of ourselves. Without this awareness, we are more vulnerable to fear, more likely to react reflexively, and in danger of mistaking the past for the present. This type of reactivity can impair our capacity to realistically adapt to what is happening in the moment. Consciousness and breath can be used to calm our physical body and shift the fight and flight response instead of reflexively reacting with alarm and sympathetic arousal. Awareness of our bodily state can help us resist automatically feeling overwhelmed by our fears in the face of a tsunami of change and existential threat. Lorie Dechar also writes about the Strength card in her wonderful book *The Alchemy of Inner Work* in the context of the right relationship between the body and the mind.[23]

The archetypal symbolism of the lion provides wisdom and guidance for these times of enormous change. Every sign of the zodiac is paired with the sign that is on the opposite side of the wheel, 180 degrees across from it. The opposite sign represents an antidote, and together, the pair forms a balanced and complete energetic whole. The sign opposite from Aquarius is Leo, the zodiac sign symbolized by the noble lion and ruled by the Sun. The evolved archetype is associated with warmth, heart centeredness, generosity, self-expression, creativity, play, the legacy we leave to our children, and courage. These beautiful qualities of mature Leo energy are ones that we can consciously choose to cultivate and embody as an antidote to the sterility, coldness, control, and anonymity of shadow Aquarius. The Strength

---

23 Lorie Dechar, *The Alchemy of Inner Work: A Guide for Turning Illness and Suffering into True Health and Well-Being* (Weiser, 2021).

card featuring the lion offers medicine for these times, and it would be useful for all of us to meditate upon the meaning and to call upon its magic during this period of radical transformation.

## Androcles and the lion

There are numerous versions of the fable of Androcles and the lion. In a version attributed to Aesop, in ancient Rome, a slave named Androcles escaped from his master and hid in the forest. One day, he came upon a massive lion lying on the forest floor, moaning in pain. The sight of the wild lion terrified Androcles, but much to his surprise, instead of leaping up to attack him, the lion held out his paw to Androcles in a gesture of asking for help. Androcles overcame his fear and gently took the lion's huge paw into his own hands. He saw that the paw was bleeding and swollen due to a thorn that was deeply embedded in it. Mustering his courage, he carefully removed the thorn. In gratitude, the lion led Androcles back to his den and, in the days that followed, fed him meat from the animals he hunted. One day, both Androcles and the lion were captured by soldiers, brought to Rome, and separated from each other. The lion was starved, to ready him to devour a prisoner in front of a crowd at the Circus Maximus. The emperor and his court eagerly anticipated a bloody spectacle, but when the lion was let loose from his cage, he bounded into the arena and up to Androcles, recognized his dear friend, and, instead of tearing him to pieces, began to lick him. When the emperor called Androcles to him and was told the whole story, he was so impressed that he pardoned Androcles and set the lion free in the forest. Aesop's fables always end with a moral. The moral of this story is "Gratitude is the sign of a noble soul."

This fable is included here because it features a lion, and the archetypal qualities commonly associated with lions such as bravery, strength, nobility, protection, and power are spiritually protective as we face the fear that is inevitable at times of massive change. Courage is a quality often associated with lions, the root of which is the Latin *cor*, meaning "heart." Real courage is not about exercising power over others or dominating with force, but, like the image in the Strength card, it is the courage to master our emotions and fears, to become intimate with the unconscious parts of ourselves, and to respond to events in the world and to others with equanimity. The lion symbolizes the courage to follow our heart and speak and act in accordance with our truth.

The moral of the fable emphasizes the virtue of gratitude. Instead of fixing our attention on a lack, on what is missing in our lives and what we wish were different, we can notice the abundance and all the blessings and really appreciate them. In the fable of Androcles and the lion, a relationship of respect and caring is portrayed. Androcles did not let his fear stand in the way of ministering to the lion. Androcles is ultimately saved by his act of compassionate service to the lion, just as Chiron was saved through the gods' reward of his act of service to Prometheus. Both stories illustrate that we ultimately save ourselves through our service to others.

The qualities represented by the Strength card—connecting the conscious and unconscious, the multidimensional and embodied, and the courage to speak my truth—have all contributed to my healing. The practices of compassion and gratitude portrayed in the tale of Androcles and the lion have also been fundamental ingredients in my alchemical healing process. Although I wish I had been ready to express myself more authentically and to spiritualize my life sooner, readiness and capacity for change only occur in accordance with divine timing. I continue to grow, change, and develop. I am a work in progress, as are all beings.

Divine timing also applies to our current planetary crisis. Human beings are apex predators. The natural history of apex predators when they become too populous is that they decimate their prey and then consequently die out themselves until the prey have a chance to regenerate. This is an ecological reality and a natural law. But we are not just apex predators. We are also spiritual beings capable of extraordinary imagination, embodied by the archetypal symbol of Chiron, capable of creative genius, skillful healing, deep love, and sacrifice. The reappearance of the white lions and their message to us at this time of crisis urge us to make use of our great capacity for imagination to avert disaster and not to blindly embrace the fate of the overpopulous apex predator.

There would be no purpose for them to warn us if there was no hope that we could change. We are at an inflection point and are being given a rare and remarkable opportunity and invitation as a species to choose between the modern mindset of human beings as separate from an inanimate Earth devoid of intelligence or a model of interdependence, interpenetration, and enchantment where we are at one with a living, conscious planet, and the Universe that exists both within and without us.

May the ideas in the book open your mind and your hearts and provide perspectives, practices, and therapies that will support your healing and offer encouragement and inspiration. May you be blessed to cultivate a loving relationship with yourself and others; to listen deeply; to notice the synchronicities; to surrender to the wisdom of your intuition, ancestors, and spirit guides; to feel intimately connected with your community and the natural world; and to experience a sense of belonging. May you trust in the unfolding great mystery and feel empowered to fulfill your heavenly mandate during these challenging and transformational times.

# ACKNOWLEDGMENTS

Gratitude to my patients who taught me so much and who allowed me to learn from them and include their stories in my book.

Gratitude to my dear friend Beata Pawska for her loving support and encouragement.

Gratitude to the generous friends who read my manuscript, Chris Allen, Betsy Mac Michael, LeAnn Plank, and Benjamin Fox.

Gratitude to my first astrology teachers Steven Forrest and Maurice Fernandez for imparting to me the precious gift of this ancient wisdom tradition.

Gratitude to my brilliant mentor Neil Nathan, MD, for teaching me to help patients with chronic complex medical conditions and for his generous support, responsiveness, and encouragement.

Gratitude for the wisdom and spiritual support I received from Carolyn Romano, Deena Metzger, Steven Vannoy, and Jamy and Peter Faust.

Gratitude to Sheila Parr who created a book cover that visually captures the essential energy of *Sacred Psychiatry* and that I love.

Gratitude to my editor, Lee Zarnikau, whose equanimity and responsivity I have so appreciated and who has had unfailingly great judgment.

# RESOURCES

The following resources can help you on your holistic journey, especially in treating the illnesses discussed in chapter 7: The website of The International Society for Environmentally Acquired Illness has a page to help you locate practitioners in your area who are literate about these conditions. Another option is to go to Neil Nathan's website; he also has a list of practitioners who have trained with him and who are knowledgeable about diagnosis and treatment of these conditions.

There are many wonderful online resources where patients with EDS can learn and exchange information with one another. A great resource is the Ehlers–Danlos Society website (www.ehlers-danlos.com), which has a Facebook group, a helpline, a YouTube channel, and webinars. It also has a list of practitioners who are EDS literate.

An excellent new book on the subject is called *Disjointed*, edited by Diana Jovin, which is a collection of chapters on various aspects of EDS written by different authors.

## Books and articles

Arrien, Angeles. *The Second Half of Life: Opening the Eight Gates of Wisdom.* Sounds True, 1998.

Arrien, Angeles. *Tarot Handbook.* Putnam, 1997.

Ashton, Heather. *The Ashton Manual.* Benzodiazepine Information Coalition, 2019.

Blank, Martin. *Overpowered: What Science Tells Us about the Dangers of Cell Phones and Other Wi-Fi Devices.* Seven Stories Press, 2015.

Broderick, Lisa. *All the Time in the World: Learn to Control Your Experience of Time to Live a Life without Limitations.* Sounds True, 2021.

Davies, James, and John Read. "A Systematic Review into the Incidence, Severity, and Duration of Antidepressant Withdrawal Effects: Are Guidelines Evidence-Based?" *Journal of Addictive Behaviors* 97 (2019): 111–121.

Dechar, Lorie. *The Alchemy of Inner Work: A Guide for Turning Illness and Suffering into True Health and Well-Being.* Weiser, 2021.

Dechar, Lorie. *Kigo: Exploring the Spiritual Essence of Acupuncture Points through the Changing Seasons.* Singing Dragon, 2021.

Forrest, Steven. *The Inner Sky: How to Make Wiser Choices for a More Fulfilling Life.* Seven Paws Press, 2012.

Frawley, David, and Vasant Lad. *An Ayurvedic Guide to Herbal Medicine.* Lotus Press, 2008.

Fung, Jason, with Jimmy Moore. *The Complete Guide to Fasting: Heal Your Body through Intermittent, Alternate-Day, and Extended Fasting.* Victory Belt, 2016.

Gervais, Michele Marie. *Spiritual Portraits of the Energy Release Points*. Tellwell Talent, 2016.

Hoffman, Edward. *The Kabbalah Deck*. Chronicle Books, 2000.

Holmes, Peter. *Aromatica: A Clinical Guide to Essential Oil Therapeutics*. Singing Dragon Press, 2019.

Laird, Eileen. *A Simple Guide to the Paleo Autoimmune Protocol*. CreateSpace, 2015.

Lamott, Annie. *Help, Thanks, Wow: Three Essential Prayers*. Riverhead Books, 2012.

Levy, Naomi. *Einstein and the Rabbi: Searching for the Soul*. Flatiron Books, 2017.

Levy, Naomi. "Learning to Take a 'Soul-fie' at Hanukah." *Hadassah Magazine* (November 2017).

Maté, Gabor, and Daniel Maté. *The Myth of Normal*. Avery, 2022.

Memon, Anjum, Imogen Rogers, Sophie M. D. D. Fitzsimmons, Ben Carter, Rebecca Strawbridge, Diego Hidalgo-Mazzei, and Allan H. Young. "Association between Naturally Occurring Lithium in Drinking Water and Suicide Rates: Systematic Review and Meta-Analysis of Ecological Studies." *Journal of Psychiatry* 217 (2020): 667–678.

Nathan, Neil. *Energetic Diagnosis: Groundbreaking Thesis on Diagnosing Disease and Chronic Illness*. Victory Belt, 2021.

Nichols, Chani. *You Were Born for This: Astrology for Radical Self-Acceptance*. HarperCollins, 2021.

Schwartz, Richard. *No Bad Parts: Healing Trauma and Restoring Wholeness*. Sounds True, 2021.

Simmons, Robert, and Naisha Ahsian. *The Book of Stones*. Heaven and Earth, 2005.

Trzeciak, Steven, and Anthony Massarelli. *Wonder Drug: 7 Scientifically Proven Ways that Serving Others Is the Best Medicine for Yourself.* St. Martin's Essentials, 2022.

Wahls, Terry. *The Wahls Protocol Cooking for Life: The Revolutionary Modern Paleo Plan to Treat All Chronic Autoimmune Conditions.* Avery, 2017.

## Webpages

The Ehlers–Danlos Society Health Care Professionals Directory: https://www.ehlers-danlos.com/healthcare-professionals-directory

The Environmental Working Group's Dirty Dozen list: https://www.ewg.org/foodnews

The Histamine Intolerance Awareness UK Food List: www.histamineintolerance.org.uk/about/the-food-diary/the-food-list

The International Society for Environmentally Acquired Illness's Find a Practitioner Page: https://iseai.org/find-a-professional

Ruth King's post "The Art of Suffering" on RuthKing.net: https://ruthking.net/the-art-of-suffering

Neil Nathan's website practitioners page: https://neilnathanmd.com/books

Loralee Scaife's blog post on Pluto and Saturn: https://www.llastrology-lotr.com/blog

# ABOUT THE AUTHOR

JUDY SUZANNE REIS TSAFRIR, MD, is a holistic healer, activist, artist, and gardener with a private practice of holistic psychiatry and psychoanalysis located in Newton, Massachusetts. She is a board-certified adult and child psychiatrist and psychoanalyst, is on the faculty of Harvard Medical School and the Boston Psychoanalytic Institute and teaches and supervises at the Cambridge Health Alliance. She has particular interest in combining spiritual and developmental approaches to healing, helping patients wean from psychiatric medications, and treating complex chronic medical conditions that present psychiatrically, including mold toxicity, mast cell activation, and Ehlers–Danlos Syndrome. Ketamine Assisted Psychotherapy (KAP) is also offered in her practice. She is a practitioner of a variety of energy healing and esoteric modalities, including flower essence therapy, aroma therapy, astrology, tarot, Shamanism, BodyIntuitive, and Reiki. Spiritually, she is drawn to Animism, Kabbalah, Buddhism, Taoism, and Quakerism. Her practice is dedicated to healing through the integration of heart, mind, body, soul, the biosphere, and the cosmos.

www.ingramcontent.com/pod-product-compliance
Lightning Source LLC
Chambersburg PA
CBHW030442090526
44586CB00044B/575